P9-DMP-166

DATE DUE

12/29/09		
JAN 2 0 2010		
2-11-10		
Mar 3		
3-26-10		
5/27		
GAYLORD		PRINTED IN U.S.A.

Ciao Italia
Five-Ingredient
FAVORITES

ALSO BY MARY ANN ESPOSITO

❖

Ciao Italia Slow and Easy

Ciao Italia Pronto!

Ciao Italia in Tuscany

Ciao Italia in Umbria

Ciao Italia: Bringing Italy Home

Ciao Italia

Nella Cucina

Celebrations Italian Style

What You Knead

Mangia Pasta!

Ciao Italia

Five-Ingredient

FAVORITES

*Quick and Delicious Recipes
from an Italian Kitchen*

Mary Ann Esposito

ST. MARTIN'S PRESS
New York

CIAO ITALIA FIVE-INGREDIENT FAVORITES. Copyright © 2009 by Mary Ann Esposito.
All rights reserved. Printed in the United States of America.
For information, address St. Martin's Press,
175 Fifth Avenue, New York, N.Y. 10010.

Photographs © 2009 by Heath Robbins

www.stmartins.com

Design by Kathryn Parise

ISBN 978-0-312-37769-4

First Edition: September 2009

10   9   8   7   6   5   4   3   2   1

To Mom,
All Your Wisdom Is Between the Pages

Contents

Acknowledgments

❧⸙❧

A s any book author knows, writing is a lonely process, but when a book comes to fruition it is because a team of unseen, dedicated professionals pulled a work of words together in a creative and artful way. I would like to thank them. First, my editor, Michael Flamini, who has guided me in the right direction by always keeping his pulse on the trends of the day, and who is always kind enough to try the recipes that I send him. He knows food! To my agent, Jane Dystel, who believed in me and worked tirelessly on my behalf, you have my utmost respect and admiration, and I count myself lucky to be among your clients. Thank you to the staff at St. Martin's Press: Vicki Lame, Jane Liddle, Leah Ransom Stewart, Kathryn Parise, Cheryl Mamaril, Jennifer Krusch, and Steve Snider. Kudos to Heath Robbins for the delicious photographs, and to Catrine Kelty for the eye-popping food styling. Who could resist trying the recipes? Thank you to my husband, Guy, always the thumbs up or thumbs down taste tester of the recipes that I cook. Your advice is always cherished. And lastly, thanks to you, dear readers, for your loyalty over the years; you keep me cooking!

Introduction

Give Me Five

When is less more? When you can turn just FIVE ingredients into something that is not only delicious but exciting, fun, and easy to make. I have known all along that one of the genius qualities of seasoned Italian cooks is the inherent ability to make something out of almost nothing; my grandmothers did it, my mother does it, and I am happy to say that it has rubbed off on me! Now I want to pass on what I have learned to you, so you can be a genius in the kitchen, too. Really. Read on!

The secret to achieving great-tasting Italian food today is in a word, *quality*. The highest-quality food products are a benchmark for Italian cooks. The brightest vegetables, the most fragrant herbs, the just-caught fish, the fruity cold-pressed olive oil, the natural grain-fed chickens, the aged artisan cheeses, the stone hearth–baked crunchy, crusted breads, and the thin-as-paper pizza, are some of the most respected Italian foods, many still made the old-fashioned way, by hand. This care and pride of workmanship is what gives Italian food its worldwide seal of approval and respect. It is no surprise then that Italian food is America's number one favorite ethnic food.

How can we translate that kind of quality to our own kitchens? By adhering to a rule that all good Italian cooks know: less is more. Everyone loves Italian food but not everyone knows that it's best not to tinker with the inherent integrity of the ingredients. Good ingredients can stand on their own with little embellishment in the seasoning and multiple ingredients department. Often just a squeeze of fresh lemon juice or a drizzle of extra-virgin olive oil is all that is needed to satisfy even the most demanding foodie. The charm lies in the fact that the ingredients are simply prepared. That is why most Italian cooks take a minimalist approach to cooking; they take their inspiration from what is local and in season. And that is why Italian food shines on its own; it is not layered, fusion, or confusion food. It is always trendy, and never tiring. Some cooks fret over the amount of time they think they need to spend prepping and cooking in order to achieve quality. They bemoan the complexity, expense, or amount of ingredients called for. It is just as easy to create a delicious dish with few ingredients as it is with an armload.

Today, we eat differently, on the run and not always together, and often, not very wisely. Yet we want unencumbered, easy-to-prepare, healthy, but delicious food. That is why this book, offering recipes with just FIVE ingredients, fits perfectly into the philosophy of Italian food. This book will deliver the results using the concept of less is more, showcasing a myriad of refreshing recipes from *antipasti* to *dolci,* using no more than FIVE ingredients. (Salt and pepper do not count.)

I have had great fun creating these recipes for you, all using ingredients readily available. And best of all, I know that the recipes will exceed your expectations, and I predict that once you try them, you will be doing high *FIVEs* across the kitchen table. *Buon Appetito!*

Five Favorite Foods
for Thought

I want you to think differently about the way you approach cooking. What if you had a limited amount of food ingredients to cook with? How would you use them? Think about where you keep food ingredients: in your cupboard or pantry, refrigerator and freezer, right? What would you consider as the five top ingredients to have in each of those locations? That will tell you a lot about the way you cook. Well, here is what I would have, and how I would use them with a little enhancement from everyday staples like salt, pepper, and flour. I can get a lot of variety from the list below by drawing on the five ingredients from the pantry, refrigerator, and freezer, proving once again that less often means more.

FIVE BASICS FROM THE PANTRY

Olive Oil
Assorted Dry Pasta
Canned Plum Tomatoes
Onions
Red Wine

Olive oil is the common denominator when it comes to Italian cooking; it is used to sauté, bake, dress salads, and drizzle over fish and meats. It is also the base for creating sauces and emulsions. No Italian kitchen is without a selection of extra-virgin olive oils, meaning oil that is derived from olives that are cold pressed and have less than 1-percent acidity. There are numerous extra-virgin olive oils, all with regional characteristics depending on climate and olive type. Like wine, you need to decide what your palate prefers. In the case of extra-virgin olive oils, there are dense and fruity ones from the south of Italy and lighter and milder tasting varieties from the central and northern areas. Buy a few bottles from different regions and try them in your cooking. Olive oil leads to the next must-have in the pantry, an assortment of dried pasta from tiny soup acini di pepe to ziti. It stands to reason that if you have olive oil, onions, and tomatoes, you can make great sauces and do wonders with these ingredients in soups, stews, and rice, vegetable, and bean dishes. And red wine is as essential for cooking as it is for enjoying with your meal. Many a dish I make, from risotto to sauces for meat to poaching liquids for baked pears, plums, and cherries, get a needed boost from red wine.

FIVE BASICS FROM THE REFRIGERATOR

Pancetta
Parmigiano-Reggiano or Pecorino Cheese
Eggs
Ricotta Cheese
Spinach or Lettuce

I always have a chunk of pancetta, unsmoked bacon, on hand. I use it to give flavor to lean cuts of meat when sautéing. I like it mixed with onions when I am making a risotto, or I use it with eggs to make a frittata. A hunk of Parmigiano-Reggiano or pecorino knows no bounds in the kitchen. Eaten out of hand with a glass of wine, it is pure heaven and the simplest antipasto when guests drop in. And if that were not enough, when it is grated it is perfect not only over pasta, but also mixed into vegetables or soups. When it is shaved, it is the perfect special something on top of a salad or in a panino. If you have eggs, you have it made; eggs are a near-perfect food; boil them, poach them, fry them, turn them into a frittata. Or make eggs in purgatory with tomato sauce and serve them on a bed of wilted spinach and supper is fine and full of richness with little effort. Ricotta cheese, what can I say; eat it as is for a healthy lunch, or serve it warm with honey and nuts for dessert; use it in fillings, or make a ricotta, Parmigiano-Reggiano, and spinach sauce for pasta. On Sunday mornings, I like to treat my family to ricotta cheese blintzes. Got lettuce? Mix the leaves with good olive oil, salt and pepper, and top with fried pancetta croutons. Throw on a sliced hard-boiled egg, and lunch is ready! And all of that is within the five basic ingredients in the fridge.

FIVE BASICS FROM THE FREEZER

Prepared Puff Pastry
Whole or Cut-up Chicken
Prepared Pizza Dough
Peas
Chicken, Vegetable, or Beef Stock

I know you are busy and that is why it is always good to have prepared puff pastry on hand. With it, you can make a chicken pot pie with onions, peas, chicken stock, cheese, and spinach. Or use it to line a pie pan with to make a torta, and fill it with a mixture of eggs, ricotta cheese, spinach, and pancetta. Frozen pizza dough can be topped with tomato sauce and cheese, or turn it into a calzone filled with ricotta, spinach, and grated Parmigiano-Reggiano and serve with tomato sauce on the side. You can make a loaf of bread or dinner rolls or bread sticks sprinkled with Parmigiano-Reggiano or pecorino cheese out of it, too!

Big Five
ANTIPASTI

Antipasto Piccante
SPICY ANTIPASTO WRAP

Spuma di Mortadella e Parmigiano-Reggiano
WHIPPED MORTADELLA AND PARMIGIANO-REGGIANO CHEESE BITES

Fonduta
ITALIAN CHEESE FONDUE

Formaggio alla Milanese
FRIED CHEESE, MILAN STYLE

Panini di Mortadella e Fontina alla Griglia
GRILLED MORTADELLA AND FONTINA CHEESE PANINI

Involtini di Prosciutto di Parma Fontina e Fichi
PROSCIUTTO DI PARMA, FONTINA, AND FIG WRAPS

Pizza di Prosciutto e Pignoli
PROSCIUTTO AND PINE NUT PIZZA

Tortine de Soppressata
SPICY SOPPRESSATA TARTLETS

Paté di Fegato alla Toscana
TUSCAN CHICKEN LIVER PATÉ

Anticipating Antipasto

What? No antipasto course? These stressful questions were aimed at me while I was preparing an anniversary dinner for an Italian couple living in Tuscany. All their friends were coming to a party, and the pressure was on. After shopping all day in the pristine outdoor market at Sasso Marconi, near the town of Polverara, I got to work prepping for the first course: plump cheese-filled tortellini to be served in broth. The second course, a succulent stuffed veal roast laced with herbs, would be served with appropriate vegetables, which I had not yet decided on, and the dessert course would be a peach and plum crostata. Emma and Franco, the honored guests, kept right on quizzing me about the menu, and as I explained it, the furrows in their brows ran deep. I had not mentioned antipasto! Unthinkable! Un-Italian and disastrous! I bowed a deep mea culpa and said *"Ma certo, faró gli antipasti."*

Antipasto, meaning to go before the meal, has always been an integral part of the Italian dining experience, and can be a small or large parade of small foods, a tasting meant to get the palate revved up for what comes next. That was then.

Times have changed in Italy since I prepared that meal. Now the antipasto bar, Italy's answer to fast food, is a huge attraction. Step into a *ristorante* these days and before your eyes lays a highway of prepared dishes, both hot and cold, including such classics as marinated seafood salad, a gallery of mixed grilled vegetables, stuffed and fried olives, succulent artichokes, eggplant involtini, marinated sardines, wafer-thin slices of prosciutto di Parma, assorted *salumi locali*, juicy herbed mushrooms, and more. This idea is taking hold in many Italian cities because time to cook a multicourse meal is a luxury, and this is a great way to get variety, value, and vindication from the kitchen! Meet your friends, sip wine, enjoy antipasto, and call it a day.

The ritual of preparing and serving antipasto may be changing, but there are subtle rules that will always remain constant. Use quality ingredients and prepare them without much embellishment. Let the character of the food shine on its own. And above all, enjoy them in an unhurried atmosphere.

FIVE ANTIPASTO TIPS

1) Variety is key and gives interest to an antipasto spread that includes such things as cold meats, marinated fish, tiny hot meatballs, and grilled vegetables.

2) Offer both hot and cold foods that can be made ahead.

3) Keep hot foods hot by using hot trays or slow cookers.

4) For an antipasto party, keep the size of food small so that no more than a fork or your fingers are needed.

5) It is always a good idea to have an identifying label for each dish in case there are allergy concerns.

Antipasto Piccante

Spicy Antipasto Wrap

- 1 large roasted and marinated sweet red bell pepper, cut into ¼-inch strips
- 8 sun-dried tomatoes in olive oil, drained, cut into pieces, oil reserved
- 4 large romaine lettuce leaves
- ½ cup grated pecorino cheese with peppercorns
- ½ cup arugula, shredded

You won't feel guilty eating this delicious, spicy, antipasto wrap! It is filled with things you would find on a typical antipasto like tomatoes in olive oil and sweet marinated bell peppers. Vary the filling, too, using eggplant, marinated zucchini, marinated mushrooms, even anchovies!

In a bowl combine the peppers, sun-dried tomatoes, and 2 tablespoons of the oil from the tomatoes. Season the mixture with salt to taste. Set aside.

Place the romaine leaves on a cutting board and divide and sprinkle the cheese evenly over each leaf. Divide and spoon the pepper-tomato mixture evenly over the cheese. Divide and sprinkle the arugula over the pepper mixture.

Roll each leaf up tightly on itself like a jelly roll. Stick a toothpick in the center of each wrap to hold it, and place on a serving dish.

This recipe can be doubled.

Makes 4

Spuma di Mortadella e Parmigiano-Reggiano

Whipped Mortadella and Parmigiano-Reggiano Cheese Bites

Spuma means whipped and a spuma of mortadella and Parmigiano-Reggiano cheese makes the perfect light spread for sweet red pepper slices or slices of ripe pears. Mortadella is a cooked pork sausage from the region of Emilia-Romagna that is studded with chunks of creamy white fat and black peppercorns, not pistachios! It is usually served in chunks as part of an antipasto, but is delicious when made into a paste for spreading on vegetables and fruits as part of a new way to serve it as an antipasto.

Grind the mortadella in a food processor until it is in coarse bits. Add the mascarpone cheese and process until a paste forms. Transfer the paste to a bowl and stir in the Parmigiano-Reggiano cheese. Season with salt to taste. Set the paste aside.

Cut the bell peppers or pears lengthwise and remove the seeds, or cores, and stems. Cut the peppers into 1-inch pieces, or the pears into ¼-inch-thick slices.

With a small spoon, spread about 2 teaspoons of the spuma on the peppers or pears. Sprinkle with the nuts. Arrange the slices on a serving dish. Serve at room temperature.

Serves 8

- ¼ pound sliced mortadella with peppercorns
- 4 ounces mascarpone cheese, at room temperature
- 3 tablespoons grated Parmigiano-Reggiano cheese
- *Fine sea salt*
- 2 large sweet red bell peppers, or two large ripe Anjou pears
- ¼ cup finely chopped pistachio nuts

❖ CHEF'S SECRET: Spuma also makes a great filling for wraps.

Fonduta

Italian Cheese Fondue

- 1 pound Italian fontina cheese, cut into bits
- 1 cup whole milk
- 2 tablespoons melted unsalted butter
- 4 large egg yolks
- One 1-pound loaf of rustic-style country bread, thickly sliced into 1-inch pieces, and toasted

Fonduta is, as its name implies, a fontina cheese dish, or fondue, from the Piedmont and Val d'Aosta regions of northwestern Italy. It is a soft, mild-tasting cow's milk cheese that is typically served as part of an antipasto with slices of toasted bread and a glass of wine. Be sure to ask for authentic Italian fontina, with its reddish brown rind, to make sure you are buying the real thing.

Combine the cheese and milk in a medium saucepan and allow it to sit, off the heat, for 2 hours.

Add the butter to the milk and cheese mixture. Cook the mixture over medium-low heat, stirring with a whisk, until the cheese is smooth. Increase the heat to medium-high and, whisking constantly, add the egg yolks one at a time, making sure that each is well incorporated before adding the next. The mixture should be very creamy.

Pour the fonduta into individual dishes or plates and surround with the pieces of toasted bread.

Serves 8

❖ CHEF'S SECRET: Soft cheeses like fontina are best cut with a serrated tomato knife, also called an angel food cake knife.

Formaggio alla Milanese

Fried Cheese, Milan Style

What could be better than a grilled cheese sandwich? How about fried cheese, without the bread? Use a good melting cheese like mozzarella or fontina.

Coat the cheese chunks in the flour then dip them twice in the beaten egg. Coat each chunk in bread crumbs.

Heat 3 cups of the oil in a deep two-quart saucepan until the temperature reaches 375°F on an instant read thermometer.

Fry the chunks in the hot oil until golden brown. Drain them on paper towels and serve hot.

Serves 4

- 8 ounces mozzarella or Italian fontina cheese, cut into thick 1-inch chunks
- All-purpose flour, for coating
- 2 large eggs, lightly beaten
- Fine dry bread crumbs, for coating
- Canola oil, for frying

Panini di Mortadella e Fontina alla Griglia

Grilled Mortadella and Fontina Cheese Panini

- ½ cup flat-leaf parsley leaves

  1 teaspoon coarse sea salt

- 1 stick (8 tablespoons) unsalted butter, at room temperature, plus 4 tablespoons

- 8 slices good-quality bread, cut into ½-inch slices

- 1 pound mortadella, thinly sliced

- ½ pound Italian fontina cheese, thinly sliced

Panini, *little sandwiches, have taken over the lunch counter! The popular way to have them is grilled, and the most important part of the sandwich is the bread! It must be of good quality, hearty, and with a tight crumb like a sourdough or whole-grain bread. A soft loaf will just fall apart. These mortadella and fontina cheese panini get extra flavor when they are spread with parsley butter. Mortadella, a pork product, is the true baloney of the region of Emilia-Romagna, and fontina is a fantastic cow's milk cheese from the Val d'Aosta region in northern Italy. Both are perfect for these sandwiches and both are readily available in your grocery store. Or use your imagination with any number of possible fillings from ham to roasted vegetables.*

Combine the parsley leaves and salt in a food processor and pulse until the leaves are coarsely ground. Add the stick of butter, and pulse for a minute or two until a smooth spread has formed. Transfer the parsley butter to a small bowl, and set it aside.

Preheat a panini maker according to the manufacturer's directions, or heat a medium nonstick frying pan over medium-high heat.

Spread 4 slices of bread with the parsley butter. Divide and top each slice with the mortadella and fontina cheese. Top each with the remaining bread slices. Place the sandwiches on the grill, a couple at a time, and grill until the bread is crusty and the cheese has melted. Serve at once.

If using a nonstick frying pan, add 2 tablespoons of the remaining butter and allow it to melt. Place as many sandwiches as will fit easily in the pan. Using a wide metal spatula, press on the sandwiches until they are browned on the bottom. Turn the sandwiches and brown the other side. Continue making sandwiches, using the remaining butter, if needed.

Makes 4

Involtini di Prosciutto di Parma Fontina e Fichi

Prosciutto di Parma, Fontina, and Fig Wraps

- 4 large romaine lettuce leaves
- 4 teaspoons honey
- ¼ pound prosciutto di Parma, thinly sliced
- ½ pound Italian fontina cheese, cut into small bits
- 4 fresh figs, each cut lengthwise into 4 thin slices
- *Fine sea salt*

Wraps are all the rage, and a healthier way to have a sandwich without a lot of extra carbo-loading bread. Take it a step further with involtini *(rolled bundles), substituting lettuce leaves for the bread! Use large romaine, Boston Bibb, or radicchio leaves to encase a filling of prosciutto di Parma, fontina, and figs.*

Prosciutto di Parma is an artisan ham, made from the hind leg of the pig and produced in specified areas of the region of Emilia-Romagna. It must meet rigid standards as to the breed of pig, how they are raised, what they are fed, how much they weigh at time of slaughter, and how they are cured. Only when all criteria have been met does a prosciutto di Parma receive its recognizable official branding, the five-pointed ducal crown.

Place the romaine leaves on a cutting board. Brush each one with a teaspoon of the honey. Place two slices of prosciutto di Parma on top of each leaf. Add four pieces of cheese and top with 4 fig slices. Sprinkle with salt to taste.

Roll each short end of the romaine leaves up tightly on itself like a jelly roll. Stick a toothpick in the center to hold it, and place the wraps on a serving dish.

Makes 4

Pizza di Prosciutto e Pignoli
Prosciutto and Pine Nut Pizza

This elegant prosciutto di Parma-topped pizza is a cinch to make when you start with store-bought pizza dough.

Combine the two doughs together in a lightly oiled bowl. Cover the bowl tightly with plastic wrap, place the bowl in a warm, but not hot, spot, and allow the dough to double in size.

Preheat the oven to 375°F.

Line two baking sheets with parchment paper and set aside.

Punch down the dough and divide it in half. Roll out each half to fit the baking sheet. Place each half on the parchment paper.

Divide the prosciutto evenly and lay the slices over each pizza dough. Divide and sprinkle the cheese over the prosciutto.

Drizzle the top of each pizza with 2 tablespoons of the oil. Sprinkle on coarse sea salt to taste.

Cover the pizzas and let them rise for 20 minutes.

Bake the pizzas for 35 to 40 minutes, or until the crust is browned and the cheese is bubbly. Ten minutes before the pizza is done, remove it from the oven, and divide and sprinkle the pine nuts or walnuts over the top, pressing them into the dough with the back of a spoon. Continue baking the pizzas for an additional 5 minutes.

Transfer the pizzas to a cutting board, cut into squares with kitchen shears, and serve warm.

Serves 8

- Two 1-pound bags of store-bought pizza dough
- 16 slices prosciutto di Parma
- 2 cups shredded scamorza or mozzarella cheese
- ¼ cup extra-virgin olive oil
- *Coarse sea salt*
- ½ cup toasted pine nuts or chopped walnuts

Tortine di Soppressata

Spicy Soppressata Tartlets

- 1 sheet prepared puff pastry, defrosted
- 1 cup diced soppressata, or other cured salame
- ¼ pound provolone cheese, diced
- 3 large eggs, lightly beaten
- 1 cup half-and-half

  ½ teaspoon fine sea salt

Soppressata is a spicy, pressed pork, cured salame that comes from Treviso in the region of the Veneto. It is eaten as an antipasto and used to flavor many cooked dishes. It sings with flavor as part of this filling for small puff pastry tartlets. Cut the tartlets into wedges to serve as part of an antipasto, or serve them individually for lunch or as a light supper entrée.

Preheat the oven to 425°F.

Roll the sheet of puff pastry into a 14-inch rectangle. Use the base of a 4-inch tartlet pan with a removable bottom as a guide to cut out 4 circles, each 5 inches in diameter.

Press and line the circles into the tartlet pans. Place the pans on a rimmed baking sheet.

Divide and spread the soppressata in the base of each tartlet shell. Divide and sprinkle the cheese on top.

In a medium bowl, whisk together the eggs, half-and-half, and salt. Divide and pour the mixture into the tartlet shells. Bake for 10 to 15 minutes, or just until the filling sets. Remove the tartlets from the oven and set aside to cool.

When the pans are cool enough to handle, remove the tartlets from the pans. Cut each tartlet into 4 wedges, and serve as part of an antipasto. Or place each one, without cutting, on individual plates, and serve with beet and orange salad (page 111).

Serves 4

Paté di Fegato alla Toscana
Tuscan Chicken Liver Paté

If you are a fan of paté you will love this Tuscan chicken liver paté that is so easy to put together. Serve it on good crusty bread.

Cut off the top dark green leaves of the leeks, down to where the lighter green color begins. Discard the dark leaves.

Trim and discard the root ends. Cut the leeks in half lengthwise and wash them well. Dry the leeks and slice them thinly crosswise.

Combine the leeks, livers, anchovies, and capers in a medium saucepan. Pour enough olive oil over the mixture just to cover it. Cover the pot and cook over low heat, stirring occasionally, until the leeks are creamy and almost dissolved.

Transfer the mixture to a food processor and puree to a smooth paste. Add salt and pepper to taste.

Store the paté in an airtight jar or container and use as a spread on crostini.

Serves 8-10

- 4 large leeks
- 4 large chicken livers
- 4 anchovy fillets in oil, drained and minced
- 2 tablespoons capers in brine, drained
- Extra-virgin olive oil
- *Fine sea salt*
- *Freshly ground black pepper*

Big Five
SOUPS

Minestra di Spinaci
SPINACH SOUP

Vellutata di Porri
CREAMY LEEK SOUP

Crema di Broccolo e Zucchine
CREAM OF BROCCOLI AND ZUCCHINI SOUP

Zuppa alla Pavese
PAVIA'S POACHED EGG SOUP

Zuppa di Fagioli alla Toscana
TUSCAN BEAN SOUP

Zuppa di Lenticchie Ditalini e Salsiccia
LENTIL, DITALINI, AND SAUSAGE SOUP

Zuppa di Paradiso
PARADISE SOUP

Zuppa di Pomodorini Porri e Riso
CHERRY TOMATO, LEEK, AND RICE SOUP

Soup Savvy

Never made soup? There are no rules, and the process could not be simpler. And if your soup savvy extends to canned varieties, I hope you'll read the fine print on the back of the label because many of them serve up megadoses of salt.

In my house soup takes shape as soon as I open the refrigerator door and clean out leftovers. Monday's veggies, last night's chicken, that small container of cooked rice, all get a new lease on taste when added to the soup pot. That's the beauty of soup. Just about anything can be thrown into the pot, even wilted lettuce! A piping hot bowl of soup is not only comforting and nourishing, but is also often a meal in itself.

Contrary to what many people think, soup does not have to start with a stock or broth made from scratch. I have made many a soup in which the primary liquid, or sometimes the only liquid, is just water in which I have wilted down aromatic vegetables like carrots, parsnips, celery, and onions. The beauty of this is that the vegetables create their own flavorful juices without a lot of fuss. Other liquids I have used include tomato juice, milk, and wine. And you can get creative adding to that things like rice, black beans, tiny pasta noodles, eggs, cheese, and lots of other items you may have in your cupboard or pantry. I even add cheese rinds to soup for extra flavor!

Say stock or broth to some people, and they seem to think this is beyond their ability. Just what is the difference between stock and broth? Well, simply put, a broth is a liquid in which vegetables, poultry, meat, or fish have been boiled. Seasonings and herbs are added to refine and round out the flavor. Broth-based soups tend to be lighter than stock-based ones. A stock, on the other hand, often begins with roasting meat or poultry bones, along with vegetables, then tossing them in a stockpot, and covering them with liquid. Long, slow simmering creates a full-bodied, dark rich stock. Broth and stock are often used to enhance the taste of sauces as well as soups. I always make enough to freeze, so I always have it on hand.

Anyone can open a can of soup, but it is far better to open your refrigerator and create your own from what you already have on hand. Once you start, there is no end to the soups you can make with just a few ingredients. Now that is being a savvy soup maker!

FIVE SOUP TIPS

1) Don't toss those meat bones, ham bones, chicken carcasses, or shrimp and lobster shells; all add flavor to soup.

2) When you have no time to make broth, use low-sodium canned varieties easily found in your supermarket and enhance them with herbs, diced vegetables, and spices.

3) Refrigerating soup overnight brings any fat to the surface, which can then be skimmed off with a spoon, and saves you hundreds of calories!

4) Drop a slightly beaten egg white into boiling broth or stock; it will foam up and act like a magnet to attract the scum that forms on top.

5) Save the liquids used to cook vegetables such as broccoli, cauliflower, and spinach and add them to soup for additional flavor and nutrition.

Minestra di Spinaci

Spinach Soup

- 1 pound fresh spinach, stemmed and washed
- 3 tablespoons unsalted butter
- 1 tablespoon all-purpose flour
- 1 quart whole milk
- ½ cup heavy cream

  Fine sea salt

  Freshly ground black pepper

This light and creamy-tasting spinach soup can be ready in minutes.

Place the spinach in a soup pot with just the water clinging to its leaves. Cover the pot, and cook the spinach over medium heat just until it is soft and wilted.

Transfer the spinach, with its liquid, to a large bowl and puree it with an immersion blender, or use a blender or food processor. Set aside.

Melt the butter in the same soup pot over medium heat. Whisk in the flour and continue whisking until a smooth paste forms. Do not let the paste brown.

Slowly whisk in the milk and continue whisking until the mixture begins to thicken slightly; stir in the spinach and heavy cream. Cook the soup over medium heat for 3 to 4 minutes. Season to taste with salt and pepper.

Serve with slices of crusty bread and shavings of Asiago Cheese.

Serves 4 to 6

Vellutata di Porri

Creamy Leek Soup

Sadly, leeks, the mild and quiet member of the onion family, do not enjoy the popularity they should. Seasoned cooks revere them for their integrity in many dishes from stews to tarts to this silky smooth leek soup.

Leeks are notoriously dirty, so first cut off the top dark green leaves down to where a lighter green color begins. Discard the dark leaves. Cut down the center of each leek; rinse them well in cold water because dirt likes to hide in all those tight folds. Then coarsely chop them.

Heat the oil in a soup pot and stir in the leeks; cook them slowly over medium heat, stirring occasionally, until they are very soft. Stir in the potatoes, cover the pot, and continue cooking until the potatoes are soft, about 5 minutes.

Add 1 cup of the broth and, off the heat, puree the mixture with an immersion blender, or transfer the mixture to a blender and process until smooth. Return the soup to the soup pot, and pour in enough additional stock to make a soup consistency. Stir in the cream and add salt and pepper to taste. Reheat the soup slowly; do not boil.

Serves 8 to 10

- 2 large leeks
- ¼ cup olive oil
- 6 medium Yukon Gold potatoes, peeled and diced
- 2 quarts low-sodium chicken broth
- 1 cup heavy cream
  Fine sea salt
  Freshly ground black pepper

Crema di Broccolo e Zucchine

Cream of Broccoli and Zucchini Soup

- 1 head broccoli, stem cut, peeled, and cut into thin strips, and broccoli separated into 1-inch florets
- 1 medium leek, white part only, sliced crosswise into rings
- 1 chicken bouillon cube
- 1 large zucchini, ends trimmed, and grated

Fine sea salt

Freshly ground black pepper

Here is a soup that can be made in any season, and the best part is that even though it is good on its own, it can make a gourmet presence on the dinner table with a topping of Parmigiano-Reggiano cheese, or a dab of fried leeks, or a trio of grilled shrimp.

Place the broccoli stems, florets, and leeks in a soup pot. Add enough water just to cover the vegetables. Add the bouillon cube.

Bring the soup to a boil, cover, and cook over medium heat until the broccoli stems are easily pierced with a knife. Add the zucchini and continue cooking, covered, for 5 minutes.

Puree the soup in batches in a blender or food processor, or use an immersion blender. Season with salt and pepper to taste. Serve hot.

Serves 4 to 6

❖ CHEF'S SECRET: Add Parmigiano-Reggiano cheese rinds to the soup while cooking for extra flavor. After cooking, cut the rinds into small "croutons" and add them back to the soup. Or serve the soup over crusty bread, and drizzle with lemon-infused olive oil. Or stir diced mozzarella cheese in to the soup just before serving.

Zuppa alla Pavese

Pavia's Poached Egg Soup

Pavia is an ancient town in southwest Lombardia that is an important fertile area for the production of dairy products, including the famous Gorgonzola cheese. Not so well-known is this nutritious soup, which can be made in minutes. Use a good country-style bread with an open crumb such as ciabatta.

Preheat the oven to 375°F.

Place the slices of toast in four individual oven-to-table soup bowls.

Crack an egg on top of each slice of toast and sprinkle each with a tablespoon of cheese. Carefully pour 1 cup of broth down the side of each bowl.

Place the bowls on a rimmed baking sheet and place the baking sheet in the preheated oven for 7 to 8 minutes, or until the eggs have just solidified and are lightly poached.

Remove the baking sheet from the oven. Sprinkle the top of the eggs with salt and pepper to taste, and serve immediately.

Serves 4

- 4 thick slices ciabatta bread, toasted and buttered
- 4 large eggs
- 4 tablespoons grated Parmigiano-Reggiano cheese
- 4 cups very hot beef or chicken broth

Zuppa di Fagioli alla Toscana
Tuscan Bean Soup

- 3 cups dried cannellini beans, soaked in water overnight
- 1 large red onion, peeled and coarsely chopped
- ½ cup fruity olive oil
- ½ cup prepared tomato sauce
- 1 quart chicken stock, plus extra as needed
- Fine sea salt
- Freshly ground black pepper

Tuscans are called mangiafagioli *(bean eaters) for their love of legumes in all forms. One favorite is cannellini beans, creamy white beans that are baked, boiled, and pureed for any number of classic dishes like this one for* zuppa di fagioli, *or bean soup. Tuscans like hearty, thick soup, but if you prefer a thinner version, add a little more water or stock.*

Drain the soaked beans. Put the beans in a large soup pot, add fresh water to cover, and bring to a boil. Stir in a teaspoon of salt, reduce the heat, and simmer the beans until their skins slip off easily. Drain the beans and set them aside.

In the same soup pot, sauté the onion in the olive oil until soft. Stir in the beans, tomato sauce, and chicken stock, and continue to cook for 30 minutes.

Puree the beans with an immersion blender, or in batches in a food mill. Return the bean puree to the pot, and add additional water or stock if needed. Season the soup with salt and pepper to taste.

Serve the soup in warm bowls with a drizzle of extra-virgin olive oil and a grating of Parmigiano-Reggiano cheese, if desired.

Serves 8-10

Zuppa di Lenticchie Ditalini e Salsiccia

Lentil, Ditalini, and Sausage Soup

Lentils are a powerhouse of protein; these tiny dried disk-shaped legumes have been used for centuries throughout the Mediterranean, and are at the heart of many Italian dishes, especially salads, soups, and casseroles. There are many varieties ranging in color from black to brown, green, reddish-brown, and yellow. It is not necessary to soak lentils before cooking, but they should be sorted and washed to remove any bits of stone or other debris. This simple lentil soup is combined with ditalini, a small tubular pasta, and Italian sausage.

Cook the sausage in a nonstick skillet over medium heat until it is no longer pink. Set aside.

Pour the chicken broth into a soup pot, add the lentils, and bring to a boil; reduce to a simmer and cook for 30 to 35 minutes. Do not overcook them or they will turn to mush; they should still have a bit of a firm core at this point.

Stir in the ditalini, and 1 teaspoon of salt and continue cooking until the pasta is almost al dente, about 5 minutes depending on the brand. Stir in the sausage and tomatoes. Cover and simmer the soup for 10 minutes. Season to taste with salt and pepper.

A salad is the only accompaniment needed as the soup is quite hearty.

Serves 8

- 3 sweet pork sausage links, casings removed and meat crumbled
- 6 cups chicken broth
- 1 cup dried lentils, sorted and washed
- ½ cup ditalini
  Fine sea salt
  Freshly ground black pepper
- 2 cups diced tomatoes

❖ CHEF'S SECRET: One cup of dried lentils yields 3 to 4 cups cooked.

Zuppa di Paradiso
Paradise Soup

- ¾ cup sifted dry bread crumbs
- ¾ cup grated pecorino or Parmigiano-Reggiano cheese
- 3 large eggs, lightly beaten
- Pinch of nutmeg
  Fine sea salt
  Freshly ground black pepper
- 2 quarts prepared chicken or beef broth

Paradise Soup is so named because who would think that tiny meatballs made solely from bread, cheese, and eggs could taste, well, so heavenly in ready-prepared chicken or beef broth. This soup tastes divine!

In a medium bowl, combine the bread crumbs, cheese, eggs, nutmeg, and salt and pepper to taste. Form into small marble-size meatballs. Set aside.

Bring the broth to a boil in a 3-quart soup pot. Reduce the heat to medium-high, add the meatballs, and cook them gently for 3 or 4 minutes. Serve hot.

Serves 8

❖ CHEF'S SECRET: When it comes to bread crumbs, the quality of the bread does make a difference. Boxed bread crumbs are but a pale imitation of the real thing. Make your own bread crumbs by drying out the pieces of stale bread in the oven on low heat. Then reduce the pieces to fine crumbs in a food processor or by hand using a rolling pin. Store the bread crumbs in an airtight container in the refrigerator.

Zuppa di Pomodorini Porri e Riso

Cherry Tomato, Leek, and Rice Soup

Even though only a few ingredients are necessary for this soup, it is very important that the tomatoes be in season for the best flavor. The secret is to use cherry tomatoes because they have few seeds and are full of sweetness. An added bonus is that it is a fat-free soup and does not contain high levels of sodium.

Cut off the top dark green leaves of the leeks down to where a lighter green color begins. Discard the green leaves. Trim and discard the root end. Cut the leeks in half lengthwise, wash them very well to remove any dirt. Cut them crosswise into thin slices. Put the leeks in a soup pot along with the tomatoes. Cover the pot, and cook, covered, over very low heat, stirring occasionally, until the tomatoes are very soft, about 10 minutes.

Puree the mixture using an immersion blender, or transfer the mixture in batches to a blender or food processor and process until very smooth.

Pour the soup in batches through a fine-mesh strainer set over a bowl, stirring the liquid and pressing on the solids with a wooden spoon to extract the juices. When the remaining pulp in the strainer is solid and dry-looking, discard it.

Return the soup to the soup pot. Stir in salt to taste, and set aside.

Meanwhile in a small saucepan, combine the rice and the water and bring to a boil. Reduce the heat to simmer, cover the pot, and

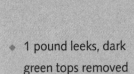

- 1 pound leeks, dark green tops removed and discarded
- 2 pounds whole cherry tomatoes
  Fine sea salt
- ½ cup long-grain white rice

cook the rice until it has absorbed all the water. Transfer the rice to the soup and stir it in. Reheat the soup and serve piping hot.

Serves 4

❖ VARIATION: Add fresh minced herbs such as parsley, basil, mint, or dill, or add diced mozzarella cheese to the soup just before serving.

Big Five
PASTA

Farfalle al Gorgonzola
BUTTERFLIES WITH GORGONZOLA
SAUCE

Fettuccine con Pecorino e Pepe Nero
FETTUCCINE WITH PECORINO
AND BLACK PEPPERCORNS

Gnocchetti al Prezzemolo
LITTLE PARSLEY GNOCCHI

Linguine alla Romana
LINGUINE ROMAN STYLE

Linguine con La Salsa di Noce
LINGUINE WITH WALNUT SAUCE

Pacco di Pasta con Pere e Taleggio
PASTA BUNDLES WITH PEARS AND
TALEGGIO

Spaghetti alla Carbonara
COAL MINERS'-STYLE SPAGHETTI

Spaghetti Integrali con Verdure Arrostite
WHOLE WHEAT SPAGHETTI WITH
ROASTED VEGETABLES

Pasta Police

Words like "pasta is bad for you," hit me hard, like a stone slung from a sling. Ever since pasta was declared a food non grata by diet gurus, it has paid a dear price in public perception. My Italian friends are more than amused when I tell them how their national dish is perceived here. We all know that too much of a good thing is not good. Italians know pasta is a good thing, and they eat it as it should be eaten, in moderation. So instead of avoiding pasta in your diet, educate yourself about it and enjoy it as the Italians do. Do you realize that one cup of cooked pasta, low in fat, low in sodium, and high in amino acids, is just 200 calories, 40 grams of carbohydrates, and no cholesterol? That would be an average serving in Italy. Here it could be (and often is) a platterful! Let's be realistic. How much pasta you eat and what you put on it are the culprits here, not the pasta itself. And remember, pasta by itself is pretty dull; think of it as a blank canvas with which you can get creative. If you follow the Italian model of a one-cup serving with tomato sauce, the added benefit is lycopene from the tomatoes, which current research seems to suggest is a cancer preventative. Even healthier is whole wheat pasta loaded with fiber and all the essential parts of the whole grain including the bran, endosperm, and the germ. Add vegetables to pasta and you're even further ahead healthwise. One of the easiest combinations is whole wheat spaghetti teamed with roasted vegetables like carrots, onions, cauliflower, or asparagus. So go ahead and blow the whistle in support of eating pasta in moderation; it's good for you!

FIVE PASTA TIPS

1) Short cuts of pasta such as rigatoni and ziti are best paired with chunky-style sauces. Thin pasta like cappellini are best paired with thinner-type sauces.

2) Adding a few tablespoons of the pasta cooking water, which is starchy, to sauces can help them adhere to pasta.

3) When making baked casseroles, it is best to undercook the pasta by 4 to 5 minutes since it will finish cooking in the oven.

4) Do not add olive oil to the cooking water to prevent sticking. Use 4 to 6 quarts of water to cook pasta and it will never stick.

5) A 4- to 5-quart pasta pot with a perforated insert is a must-have tool in your kitchen for cooking pasta correctly.

Farfalle al Gorgonzola
Farfalle with Gorgonzola Sauce

- ½ stick (4 tablespoons) unsalted butter
- 4 large shallots, peeled and minced
- 2 cups crumbled Gorgonzola dolce cheese
- ½ cup heavy cream
  Freshly ground black pepper
- 1 pound farfalle
  Fine sea salt

Farfalle *(butterflies) refers to a type of dried pasta, also commonly referred to as bow ties. Usually tossed with tomato sauce, this pasta provides predictable and satisfying comfort food. But add a few ingredients like Gorgonzola cheese and cream, and farfalle is not just pasta anymore, but a luxurious gourmet dish. The cheese, a cow's milk cheese with blue veining, is made in Gorgonzola, a town in Lombardia in northern Italy. There is* Gorgonzola dolce *(sweet) and* Gorgonzola forte *(aged). In this dish, the sweet version is perfect.*

Melt the butter in a large sauté pan, add the shallots, and cook until softened. Reduce the heat, and add the cheese, stirring to melt it evenly until smooth. Add the cream slowly. Season with freshly ground pepper. Cover the pan, and keep the sauce warm while the farfalle cooks.

Cook the farfalle in 4 quarts of rapidly boiling water to which 1 tablespoon of salt has been added. Cook until the farfalle is al dente. This means that the farfalle is done when a piece broken in half reveals no uncooked flour in the center.

Drain and add the farfalle to the sauté pan with the gorgonzola sauce. Toss gently over medium heat to coat the farfalle with the sauce. Transfer the pasta to a serving platter. Give a good twist of the peppermill over the top, and serve hot.

Serves 8

❖ VARIATION: For an even tastier dish, stir in 6 to 8 sage leaves, torn, to the shallots before adding the cheese. Use some extra sage for garnish.

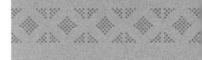

Fettuccine con Pecorino e Pepe Nero

Fettuccine with Pecorino and Black Peppercorns

- 6 tablespoons unsalted butter
- 4 tablespoons extra-virgin olive oil
- 1 pound fettucine
- ¼ pound pecorino cheese with black pep-percorns, grated

Fine sea salt

Pecorino is sheep's milk cheese. Beautifully made in many regions of Italy, when it is aged, it develops a salty taste that enhances many dishes. Pecorino with whole black peppercorns is another thing altogether. Not only is the saltiness there but also the wonderful spicy bite of pepper, which is all that is needed to pump up the flavor of this quick-to-make pasta dish.

Melt the butter in a small saucepan; add the olive oil and keep the mixture warm.

Cook the fettuccine in 4 to 6 quarts of rapidly boiling water to which 1 tablespoon of salt has been added until al dente. The pasta is done when a strand broken in half reveals no uncooked flour in the center.

Drain the fettuccine.

Pour the warm butter and olive oil onto a shallow platter; toss the fettuccine in the sauce. Sprinkle the cheese over the top, and toss again. Salt sparingly, and serve immediately.

Serves 6 to 8

❖ CHEF'S SECRET: The new thinking on how to store aged cheeses such as pecorino or Parmigiano-Reggiano is to double wrap them in plastic wrap and store in the cheese drawer of the refrigerator.

Gnocchetti al Prezzemolo

Little Parsley Gnocchi

- 2 sticks (½ pound) unsalted butter
- 1 large bunch leeks, white part only, thoroughly washed and thinly sliced crosswise
- 2 pounds Russet potatoes
- 1 to 1½ cups semolina flour
  - *1 teaspoon fine sea salt*
- ½ cup finely minced flat-leaf parsley

These little potato and parsley dumplings are so easy to make, and they make a perfect first course. Use mature baking potatoes such as Russet. They are drier in texture so less flour will be needed, resulting in lighter-tasting gnocchi.

Melt the butter in a large saucepan; stir in the leeks and cook them over medium heat until they are very creamy, about 20 minutes. Cover the pan, and keep the sauce warm.

Pierce the potatoes in several places with a small knife and microwave uncovered on high power according to manufacturer's directions. When cool enough to handle, peel and rice them into a bowl. Add the flour a little at a time, along with the salt, to create a ball of dough that holds together. Work in the minced parsley.

Divide the dough into 4 pieces; roll each piece into a 14-inch-long rope the thickness of your middle finger. Cut the rope into ½-inch pieces, and roll each piece off the tines of a floured fork. Place the gnocchetti in single rows on floured towels.

Bring 4 quarts of water to a boil. Add the gnocchetti a dozen at a time and cook until they bob to the top. Remove them with a slotted spoon to the saucepan with the melted butter and leek sauce. Continue cooking the remaining gnocchetti.

When all the gnocchetti are cooked, toss them in the sauce over low heat until well coated. Serve immediately.

Serves 6 to 8

Linguine alla Romana

Linguine Roman Style

Linguine, or little tongues, is thin, flat, ribbon pasta that is perfect with a quick sauce made with ricotta cheese. This dish comes from Rome.

Cook the linguine in 4 quarts of rapidly boiling water to which 1 tablespoon of salt has been added until it is al dente. A strand of pasta when broken in half will reveal no uncooked flour in the center.

Meanwhile combine the ricotta cheese with the butter in a saucepan and cook over low heat, stirring constantly, for about 8 minutes.

Drain the linguine, reserving ¼ cup of the pasta water, and return the linguine to the pot. Over low heat, stir in the ricotta sauce and the reserved water. Season with salt and pepper to taste. Stir in half of the cheese.

Transfer the linguine to a serving dish; pass the remaining cheese on the side.

Serves 4 to 6

- 1 pound linguine
- ½ pound whole milk ricotta cheese
- 1 stick (8 tablespoons) unsalted butter, softened
- ¼ cup cooking water from the linguine

  Fine sea salt

  Freshly ground black pepper
- ½ cup grated pecorino cheese

Linguine con La Salsa di Noce
Linguine with Walnut Sauce

- 1½ cups walnut halves
- ½ cup extra-virgin olive oil
- 4 garlic cloves, finely minced
- ½ cup finely minced flat-leaf parsley
- 1 pound linguine
- *Fine sea salt*
- *Freshly ground black pepper*

My mother learned to make walnut sauce from her mother, my grandmother, Anna Galasso. Grandma came from a small town near Avellino in the region of Campania called Bellizzi, an area noted for its nut trees, especially hazelnuts and walnuts, so naturally she made do with what ingredients were at her disposal. Walnut sauce is not only delicious, it is good for you, and takes but a few minutes to make. It is best served over linguine.

Toss the walnuts in a large sauté pan over medium heat, and toast them until they are fragrant. Be careful not to burn them, or you will be starting over! Transfer the nuts to a cutting board or to the bowl of a food processor; mince, or pulse, them until fine. Transfer them to a small bowl and set aside.

In the same sauté pan, heat the olive oil over medium heat until it begins to shimmer. Stir in the garlic and cook, pressing on the garlic with a wooden spoon to release its flavor; do not let the garlic get too brown. Reduce the heat to low, stir in the parsley, and season to taste with salt and pepper. Stir in the walnuts, cover, and keep the sauce warm while cooking the linguine.

Cook the linguine in 4 to 6 quarts of rapidly boiling water to which 1 tablespoon of salt has been added until al dente. (Fish out a strand of linguine and break it in half. Do you see any uncooked white flour in the center? If so, the linguine needs to cook longer, just until no more white flour shows when a string is broken in half.)

Drain the linguine and immediately add it to the walnut sauce. Increase the heat to medium, and stir to coat the linguine well with the sauce. If the pan seems dry, add a bit more olive oil. Serve hot.

Serves 6 to 8

Pacco di Pasta con Pere e Taleggio

Pasta Bundles with Pears and Taleggio

Using wonton wrappers for the "pasta," and ripe pears and creamy Taleggio cheese for the filling, makes this dish truly spectacular.

Gently mix the pears and Taleggio in a bowl.

Place a scant teaspoon of the filling in the center of each wonton wrapper. Bring up the four corners and twist them together to make a bundle. Set the bundles aside.

Bring 4 to 6 quarts of salted water to a boil in a pasta pot. Add the bundles and cook them until they are al dente, about 4 minutes.

Meanwhile melt the butter in a small saucepan, stir in the Parmigiano-Reggiano, and keep the mixture warm.

Carefully remove the bundles from the water with a slotted spoon and place them in a large bowl. Add the warm butter mixture, and toss the bundles gently until they are well coated. Serve hot.

Serves 8

- 3 large Anjou pears, peeled and diced
- ½ pound Taleggio cheese, cut into small bits
- 1 package wonton wrappers
  Salt
- 1 stick (8 tablespoons) unsalted butter
- ½ cup grated Parmigiano-Reggiano cheese

Spaghetti alla Carbonara
Coal Miners'-Style Spaghetti

- 1 tablespoon extra-virgin olive oil
- 4 ounce chunk pancetta, diced

  Fine sea salt
- ½ pound spaghetti
- 3 large eggs, at room temperature and lightly beaten
- ¾ cup grated Parmigiano-Reggiano cheese

  Coarsely ground black pepper

Just about everyone I know has a recipe for spaghetti alla carbonara. This simple but heavenly dish is said to get its name from the coal miners who could make it easily with readily available ingredients: eggs, cheese, and guanciale, cured and salted pig's jowl and cheeks. A likely story, but the fact is that this dish is easy to make, superb when made correctly, and a completely balanced meal. The eggs should be of the highest quality and at room temperature so they will mix well with the spaghetti. The cheese should be none other than the true Parmigiano-Reggiano, or pecorino Romano. Today, the more readily available pancetta is used in place of guanciale. And a pepper mill is absolutely essential for the right grind of black pepper.

Heat the olive oil in a small sauté pan, stir in the pancetta, and cook until crispy. Set aside the pancetta, still in the pan, and keep it warm.

Cook the spaghetti in 4 quarts of rapidly boiling salted water. Al dente means still firm to the bite but no uncooked flour is visible in the center when a strand of the spaghetti is broken in half.

Drain the spaghetti, reserving 2 tablespoons of the water. Immediately return the spaghetti to the pot and, keeping the heat very low, rapidly stir in the eggs, reserved water, and half the cheese. Toss to combine. Add the reserved pancetta and any pan drippings. Stir well. Add a generous grinding of coarse black pepper. Transfer the pasta to a platter and sprinkle it with the remaining cheese. Serve immediately.

Serves 4

Spaghetti Integrali con Verdure Arrostite
Whole Wheat Spaghetti with Roasted Vegetables

Whole wheat pasta is front and center in the pasta aisle as more people discover not only its nutty flavor but its health benefits as well. Pasta companies have heard the call and are churning out whole wheat pasta in all sorts of shapes and sizes from soup pasta to lasagne sheets. Teamed with roasted vegetables, this dish is about as healthy as it gets.

Preheat the oven to 375°F.

Pour ⅓ cup of the olive oil in a large bowl. Add 1 teaspoon salt and a grinding of pepper. Separately toss each of the vegetables—the carrots, brussels sprouts, and bell peppers—in the oil, coating them well.

Transfer the vegetables to a baking sheet and bake them in the preheated oven until a knife is easily inserted into them, about ten minutes. Keep them covered and warm while the spaghetti is cooking.

Bring 4 to 6 quarts of water to a boil. Stir in 1 tablespoon of salt. Stir in the spaghetti, pushing it down into the water with a wooden spoon. Cook the spaghetti until a strand broken in half does not reveal any uncooked flour in the center. Drain the spaghetti and return it to the pot. Over low heat, stir in the remaining ⅓ cup olive oil, and add the roasted vegetables. Heat, stirring, until everything is very hot, then transfer the mixture to a serving platter.

Serves 6-8

- ⅔ cup extra-virgin olive oil
  Fine sea salt
  Freshly ground black pepper
- 4 medium carrots, peeled and cut into ½-inch-thick rounds
- 8 brussels sprouts, trimmed and cut in half
- 2 medium sweet red bell peppers, stemmed, seeded, and cut into ½-inch-thick slices
- 1 pound whole wheat spaghetti

Big Five
SAUCES

Pesto al Peperoncino

HOT RED PEPPER PESTO

Salsa Aglio e Olio con Noci e Pecorino

GARLIC, OIL, WALNUT, AND PECORINO SAUCE

Salsa di Finocchio e Pomodorini

ROASTED FENNEL AND CHERRY TOMATO SAUCE

Salsa al Limone

LEMON SAUCE

Salsa di Olive Nere

BLACK OLIVE SAUCE

Ragù ai Funghi

MUSHROOM RAGU

Salsa Verde

GREEN SAUCE

It's in the Sauce

My anathema to commercially prepared sauces in a jar runs deep. Full of preservatives and artificial ingredient names that I cannot pronounce, it seems ludicrous to invest money and uncertainty in jarred sauces with an eternal shelf life. Fresh sauces on the other hand, bear no taste resemblance to anything from a jar. Their vibrancy gives not only flavor, but moisture and visual appeal to any dish requiring them, and the health benefits are certain. Master, or "mother sauces," fall into these categories: white stock, brown stock, tomato, milk, butter, and wine sauces. But there are many others like fish and vegetable stock-based sauces. And in Italian cooking, there are no rules when it comes to making a sauce. Liquids such as broth, wine, milk, and citrus juice are all common ingredients that can become the basis for a great sauce, as well as aromatic vegetables like carrots, celery, onions, and fresh herbs and spices. You are only limited by your imagination.

FIVE SAUCE TIPS

1) Do not use nonstick pans for making meat and poultry-based sauces. It will be hard to caramelize these ingredients in nonstick pans and this is where deep flavor resides.

2) Reducing a sauce (decreasing the volume of liquid in a pan, usually by half) will produce a sauce with a full concentration of flavors.

3) Add fresh herbs at the end of the cooking; this will help to preserve their natural oils and result in a more intense flavor.

4) A whisk is the best tool for making sauces and keeping them smooth.

5) Plastic squeeze bottles are perfect for garnishing dishes with small amounts of savory or sweet sauces.

Pesto al Peperoncino

Hot Red Pepper Pesto

Say pesto *and most people will think of the classic basil, pine nut, oil, and garlic-based sauce. But today's pestos go far beyond that, like this fiery and fabulous hot red pepper pesto. Use it on pasta, or vegetables. Spread it on pizza and crostini, but don't eat it straight from the jar! This sauce is a perfect way to use up those hot red pepper plants from the garden, or a bagful from your farmer's market! Makes a nice hostess gift as well.*

Caution is called for when handling hot peppers; it is best to wear disposable gloves and never put your hands to your eyes or face when working with hot peppers.

Place the peppers in a food processor and coarsely grind them. Add the salt, vinegar, and sugar. With the motor running, drizzle the olive oil through the feed tube until the mixture is a paste consistency.

Transfer the mixture to a jar, cap, and refrigerate. The pesto will keep for several months.

Depending on your taste, use a teaspoon to mix into chili, tomato sauce, or add it to stir-fries and sautéed mixed vegetables.

Makes one 8-ounce jar

- 12 small hot red peppers, stems removed
  1 teaspoon fine sea salt
- 1 tablespoon white balsamic vinegar
- 1 teaspoon sugar
- Extra-virgin olive oil

Salsa Aglio e Olio con Noci e Pecorino

Garlic, Oil, Walnut, and Pecorino Sauce

- 1 cup fruity extra-virgin olive oil
- 2 garlic cloves, finely minced

  1 teaspoon salt

  Freshly ground black pepper
- ⅓ cup minced flat-leaf parsley leaves
- ½ cup minced walnuts
- ¼ cup grated pecorino cheese

If there is a sauce more classic than tomato it has got to be aglio e olio, *garlic and oil sauce, and who does not have those two healthy ingredients on hand? This sauce exudes comfort; it is what I crave when I want something light, something that is not an assault on my stomach, and something that just plain puts me in a good mood. This sauce is sheer perfection and a really great example of using the best ingredients for tasty results. Use a good, fruity extra-virgin olive oil, fresh garlic, and fresh flat-leaf parsley. It is that simple. But if you want to take it one step further, add minced walnuts and pecorino cheese.*

This recipe makes enough to dress a pound of spaghetti or linguine, and can easily be doubled to serve more.

Heat the olive oil slowly over medium-low heat in a 12-inch sauté pan. When the oil begins to shimmer at the edges, stir in the garlic and cook, pressing on it with a wooden spoon, until the garlic begins to turn golden brown; take care not to let it burn, or you will have to start over.

Turn off the heat, and stir in the salt, pepper, parsley, walnuts, and cheese. Keep the sauce warm while cooking your pasta.

Makes 1¾ cups

❖ CHEF'S SECRET: Use a Microplane grater to mince garlic; just grate unpeeled cloves where you need it; the thin outer papery layer of the cloves is left behind.

Mince fresh parsley, and divide and wrap portions of 4 tablespoons tightly in a paper towel. Then fold each of them like an envelope, and freeze in small sandwich bags. That way you always have fresh parsley on hand.

Salsa di Finocchio e Pomodorini

Roasted Fennel and Cherry Tomato Sauce

- 2 tablespoons extra-virgin olive oil
- 1 large fennel bulb (about 12 ounces), bulb part only, thinly sliced into rings
- 2 pints cherry tomatoes
- 3 garlic cloves, peeled and cut in half lengthwise
- ½ teaspoon fine sea salt
- 2 teaspoons sugar

When is a sauce not just a sauce? When it can be used as a side vegetable dish, or even as a topping for pizza. Three variations in one is what you will get with this fix-it-and-forget-it roasted fennel and cherry tomato sauce. The exquisite flavor is due to one key ingredient—sugar.

Preheat oven to 350°F.

Brush a 12-inch rimmed baking sheet with the olive oil.

Add all the ingredients to the pan and toss well to coat them in the oil.

Bake the vegetables for 20 to 25 minutes, stirring occasionally, just until they have softened.

Use the sauce to dress three-quarters of a pound of spaghetti or short cut macaroni, like ziti or penne. Or use it as a topping for pizza, over baked fish, or serve as a side dish. However you use it, it is delicious!

Makes about 1¾ cups

❖ CHEF'S SECRET: Adding a tablespoon of minced capers at the end of the cooking gives a nice sweet-and-sour taste. Adding two tablespoons of chopped fresh thyme is also a refreshing variation.

Salsa al Limone
Lemon Sauce

There is nothing that perks up flavors like lemons, but why think just a squirt of lemon juice will do when this easy-to-make, velvety lemon sauce is more interesting and elegant. Use it on everything from sliced fresh tomatoes and fresh asparagus, to grilled chicken, fish, or pork. It is perfect on roasted brussels sprouts, too! Keep a jar in the refrigerator at all times.

Put the lemon segments, sugar or honey, salt, and pepper in a food processor or blender, and pulse to a coarse consistency. Pour in the olive oil and whirl until the mixture is almost smooth, leaving a little texture.

Transfer the sauce to a jar and store in the refrigerator. The sauce will keep for three to four weeks. To use, reheat slowly.

Makes about 1 cup

- 4 large lemons, peeled and segmented
- 1¼ teaspoons sugar or honey
  1 teaspoon fine sea salt
  Freshly ground black pepper
- ½ cup extra-virgin olive oil

❖ CHEF'S SECRET: The best way to store whole lemons is to keep them in a sealed jar of water. They will stay plump and yield much more juice than if they were stored dry.

Salsa di Olive Nere

Black Olive Sauce

- 7 tablespoons extra-virgin olive oil
- 1 medium onion, peeled and diced
- ½ cup pitted and chopped black oil-cured olives (about 27 olives)
- 3 plum tomatoes, peeled, seeded, and diced
  Fine sea salt
  Freshly ground black pepper
- 1 tablespoon chopped flat-leaf parsley

Prepare this pungent olive sauce early in the day and let it sit at room temperature so the flavors develop. I serve it over farfalle, butterfly-shaped pasta, but any short cut of macaroni will do.

Heat the olive oil in a medium saucepan. Add the onion and stir over medium heat until it has softened. Add the olives, tomatoes, salt, and pepper. Stir the mixture well and let it simmer, covered, for 10 minutes.

Turn off the heat, add the parsley, and stir to blend. Let the sauce sit at room temperature for several hours. When ready to use, reheat the sauce. Use it on pasta, fish, or pork.

Makes 1¼ cups

❖ CHEF'S SECRET: The best way to pit olives is to smash them with a meat pounder or a one-pound can.

Ragù ai Funghi
Mushroom Ragu

Earthy mushrooms, slow cooked in butter, make a wonderful side dish to steak or a sauce for pasta or risotto. For this simple ragù, try oyster mushrooms, which lend a velvety texture and a mild flavor to the sauce. For a bolder taste, try shiitake or cremini mushrooms. This ragù is the perfect topping for slices of grilled polenta, too. To maximize the flavor of the mushrooms, be patient; do not be in a hurry to stir them while they cook. Leave them alone and allow them to cook gently without stirring. Your patience will be rewarded.

Melt the butter in a medium sauté pan; stir in the thyme and shallots and cook them over medium heat until the garlic is soft and the mixture smells fragrant. Add the mushrooms and cook over medium-high heat, without stirring, until the mushrooms begin to release their liquid. Stir once and continue cooking until all the liquid from the mushrooms has evaporated.

Slowly pour in the cream and mix well to combine. Cover the pan, reduce the heat to low, and cook, covered, for about 5 minutes. Uncover the pan, season the ragù with salt to taste and a generous grinding of black pepper.

Makes about 2 cups

- 6 tablespoons unsalted butter
- 2 heaping tablespoons fresh thyme leaves, chopped
- 2 medium shallots, peeled and minced
- 1 pound oyster or shiitake mushrooms, wiped with a damp paper towel, and thinly sliced
- ⅔ cup heavy cream
- *Fine sea salt*
- *Freshly ground black pepper*

❖ CHEF'S SECRET: Never store mushrooms in plastic bags or plastic wrap—mushrooms need to breathe. Store them in paper bags in the refrigerator and use within two days of purchase.

Salsa Verde

Green Sauce

- 2 sticks (16 table-spoons) unsalted butter, at room temperature
- 4 garlic cloves, minced
- ½ cup coarsely chopped walnuts
- 1½ cups packed flat-leaf parsley leaves
  - ½ teaspoon fine sea salt
  - Freshly ground black pepper
- 3 to 4 tablespoons extra-virgin olive oil

Salsa verde, *(green sauce) is made with fresh parsley, basil, extra-virgin olive oil, salt, and pepper. It is a great partner to grilled eggplant or zucchini, and equally as good as a sauce for spaghetti; I also like it on grilled fish, and mixed into risotto. This is best made in a food processor.*

Put all the ingredients, except the olive oil, in the bowl of a food processor fitted with the steel blade. Process until the mixture is smooth. With the motor running, pour just enough of the oil through the feed tube to create a creamy, thick, fluid sauce.

Transfer the sauce to a jar, and store in the refrigerator. Use within a week; as the sauce sits it tends to become brown if the jar is not airtight.

Makes about 1¼ cups

Big Five
MEAT AND POULTRY

Abbacchio al Forno alla Romana

ROAST LAMB, ROMAN STYLE

Bistecca con Salsa di Capperi

STEAK WITH CAPER SAUCE

Polpettoni al Formaggio

CHEESY STUFFED MEATBALLS

Cotolette di Agnello Panate

BREADED SPRING LAMB CHOPS

Maiale al Barolo

PORK LOIN IN BAROLO WINE

Cotolette di Maiale al Pistacchio

PISTACHIO-DUSTED PORK CHOPS

Pollo in Salsa Agrodolce

SWEET-AND-SOUR CHICKEN AND EGGPLANT

Pollo al Diavolo

DEVILISH CHICKEN

Pollo al Limone ed Erbe

ROAST CHICKEN WITH LEMON AND HERBS

The Main Event

Like other chefs, I have had my share of cooking challenges. And most of them have taken place in kitchens that I have taught in in Italy. Let me give you a case in point about a "fresh meat" class I gave. One day in Rome, before my students were to arrive for a lesson on how to make a classic roasted lamb dish, *abbacchio al forno*, flavored with white wine, garlic, and rosemary, I was going over the *mise en place* (ingredients I would need) with the sous chef. "Is the lamb here?" I asked. *"Si, signora!"* Out he went to get it. When I turned in his direction, I saw him wheel in what looked like a deep laundry bin on wheels. *"Ecco l'agnello."* (Here is the lamb.) When I took a look, a whole, skinned baby lamb lay in the bin with hooves shooting upright! I was not anticipating cutting up the entire animal to get my leg of lamb, but when you ask for fresh meat in Italy, they take you seriously! Sensing that the students would not be comfortable watching an entire animal being cut into pieces, I told the chef to wheel the bin into a separate cooking area where we could cut it in private. Finally getting to the meat of the matter, I had my leg of lamb, and proceeded to prepare it for the class using only a few additional choice ingredients. What emerged from the oven was astoundingly good. It tasted more than delicious, and was an epiphany for the students because they began to realize that intricate food preparation does not necessarily guarantee success. Only the integrity of the ingredients used do, and the ability of the cook to know how not to tamper with them. The operative word here was fresh. In Italy, that does not mean a supermarket, plastic-wrapped package of precut meat with a sell date.

The following day's class was going to be about another classic, *coniglio,* or rabbit, and I was more than prepared for the task that lay ahead. Enough said.

FIVE MEAT AND POULTRY TIPS

1) Invest in an instant-read thermometer to give accurate temperature readings so you know when meat and poultry are safely cooked.

2) Refrigerate meat and poultry dishes as soon as they are cooked, if not using immediately. Do not let cool first. Place the finished dishes on a trivet or towel on the refrigerator shelf.

3) Buy organic whenever possible, which means animals have been humanely treated, have not been injected with artificial hormones, and have been fed an all-grain, natural diet.

4) Use leftover cooked meats and poultry within three days, or freeze for future use in casseroles or stir-fry dishes.

5) Buy flexible plastic cutting mats to use when working with raw meat or poultry. This will prevent contamination of your counter surfaces. The mats are dishwasher-safe and reusable.

Abbacchio al Forno
alla Romana

Roast Lamb, Roman Style

- One 4-pound leg of lamb
- 3 garlic cloves, slivered
- 3 tablespoons fresh rosemary leaves
- ½ cup extra-virgin olive oil

  1 tablespoon fine sea salt

  1½ teaspoons coarsely ground black pepper
- 1 cup dry white wine

Roast baby lamb, considered a delicacy, takes the place of honor on the Italian table. The word abbacchio *refers specifically to milk-fed, baby lamb, weighing between 15 and 25 pounds. Lamb is prepared in many ways in Italy; grilled on a spit, braised, stewed, and roasted in the oven. The Romans take particular pride in their method of cooking lamb.*

Wipe the meat dry with paper towels. With a small knife, make slits about 1-inch deep all over the meat, and insert the slivers of garlic and rosemary leaves.

In a small bowl, combine the olive oil, salt, and pepper and mix well with a fork. Rub the mixture all over the lamb, coating it well. Place the meat in a deep dish or other nonreactive container, cover it, and let it marinate in the refrigerator for 2 to 3 hours.

Preheat the oven to 350°F.

Place the lamb on a rack in a roasting pan, and add the wine to the pan. Roast the lamb for 1 to 1½ hours, until the internal temperature reaches 160°F for medium, basting the meat every 15 minutes with the pan juices. Transfer the roast to a cutting board and let it rest for ten minutes, covered loosely with foil.

Carve the lamb into pieces, arrange on a platter, and pour the pan juices over the meat. Garnish with rosemary sprigs. Serve immediately.

Serves 8

Bistecca con Salsa di Capperi

Steak with Caper Sauce

Capers are the secret gem in this tangy lemon sauce for steak. It is always amazing to me how a little pungent flower bud from a plant that grows in crags and rocks in the Mediterranean can provide such flavor, but there it is, plain and simple. The best capers come from the island of Pantelleria off Sicily.

Rub the steak with salt and pepper and allow it to sit at room temperature for 30 minutes.

Pour the olive oil into a large sauté pan, add the onions, and cook over low heat for about 10 minutes, stirring occasionally. Transfer the onions to a bowl. Increase the heat to medium-high, and add the steak to the pan. Brown the meat on both sides. Reduce the heat to medium, and stir in the capers and lemon juice. Cook to desired doneness.

Serve the steak with some of the pan juices drizzled over the top.

Serves 6 to 8

- 4 pounds Porterhouse or sirloin steak, cut ¾ inch thick
  Fine sea salt
  Freshly ground black pepper
- ⅓ cup extra-virgin olive oil
- 2 large red onions, peeled and coarsely chopped
- 3 tablespoons capers packed in salt, well rinsed and minced
- Juice of 3 large lemons

Polpettoni al Formaggio
Cheesy Stuffed Meatballs

- ½ cup good-quality dried bread crumbs
- ⅓ cup heavy cream or half-and-half
- ½ pound ground chuck
- ½ pound ground sirloin

  1½ teaspoons fine sea salt

  Coarsely ground black pepper
- ½ pound Italian fontina or mozzarella cheese, cut into 8 small pieces

Can you make a better-tasting meatball? Absolutely! Just stuff them with a creamy, melting cheese like Italian fontina! This may be a slightly unconventional way to make them, but the taste elevates the meatballs to elegant; they can be served alone or in a tomato sauce. To achieve great flavor, use a combination of ground chuck and ground sirloin. The fat in ground chuck is essential for moistness while the sirloin provides great texture.

Preheat the oven to 350°F.

Put the bread crumbs in a medium bowl and pour the cream over them. Mix with a fork; the mixture will not be soupy.

Add the ground chuck, sirloin, and salt and pepper. Mix with a fork or your hands just to combine the ingredients. Divide the mixture into 8 equal pieces and roll each in the palms of your hands to make compact 2½-inch balls.

Insert your thumb into the middle of each meatball and push in a piece of cheese. Close the meatball, encasing the cheese, and smooth the top.

Place the meatballs on a rimmed, nonstick baking sheet. Bake in the preheated oven for 20 to 25 minutes, or until they are nicely browned. Serve hot as is, or add them to a tomato sauce and serve them with pasta or as a second course.

Makes 8 meatballs

❖ VARIATION: Make the meatballs miniature size and bake them for 10 to 12 minutes. Serve as an antipasto. Leftovers make great sandwich filling, too!

❖ CHEF'S SECRET: If you wet your hands with cold water between making each meatball, the meat mixture will not stick to your hands.

Cotolette di Agnello Panate

Breaded Spring Lamb Chops

- 2 large eggs

  Fine sea salt

  Freshly ground black pepper

- 2 pounds very lean lamb loin chops, cut ¼ inch thick

- 1 cup panko or other dry bread crumbs

- ½ cup vegetable oil

- 2 lemons, cut into wedges

Crunchy Japanese bread crumbs, called panko, are used to coat these spring lamb loin chops because they deliver a nice crunchy texture. Panko are large flaky crumbs made from crustless bread. They can be readily found in grocery stores. To be sure that the bread crumbs adhere well, refrigerate the chops, uncovered, for 30 minutes before pan-frying them. The "air drying" will seal the deal.

Lightly beat the eggs with salt and pepper. Dip each chop in the egg and coat with bread crumbs. Place the chops on a dish and refrigerate, uncovered, for 30 minutes.

In a large sauté pan, heat the oil over medium-high heat until it begins to shimmer. Pan-fry the chops until browned on each side, 3 to 4 minutes.

Transfer the chops to a serving dish; arrange the lemon wedges around the edge of the dish. Serve hot.

Serves 4

> ❖ CHEF'S SECRET: When frying, use a sauté pan large enough to accommodate the chops without crowding them. Too small a pan will cause the chops to steam rather than brown.

Maiale al Barolo
Pork Loin in Barolo Wine

Barolo is one of the classic red wines of the Piedmont region of Italy and is made near the town of Alba. It is wonderful with cheese and even barbecue and it flavors this pork loin beautifully. Pour yourself a glass while the meat is cooking.

Mince the garlic and rosemary together. Place the mixture in a small bowl, and add salt and pepper. Rub the mixture all over the pork roast.

Place a Dutch oven or other heavy-bottomed, large casserole, just large enough to hold the meat, over medium-high heat. When the pan is hot, add the roast and brown it in its own fat. Pour in 1 cup of the wine, reduce the heat to simmer, cover, and cook until most of the wine has evaporated. Turn the meat once or twice halfway through the cooking process.

Combine the tomato paste with the remaining wine and add it to the pot. Cover and simmer about 1½ hours, or until the meat is tender.

Transfer the meat to a cutting board; allow it to rest, covered, loosely in aluminum foil, for 10 minutes before slicing. Cut the roast into ¼-inch slices. Return the slices to the pot and reheat and serve with some of the pan juices.

Serves 8-10

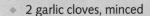

- 2 garlic cloves, minced
- 2 tablespoons fresh rosemary leaves
  1½ teaspoons fine sea salt
  ¼ teaspoon coarsely ground black pepper
- One 5-pound boneless pork loin roast
- 2 cups Barolo wine
- ½ cup tomato paste

Cotolette di Maiale al Pistacchio

Pistachio-Dusted Pork Chops

- 2 large eggs
- ¼ cup finely minced fresh rosemary leaves
  Fine sea salt
  Freshly ground black pepper
- 4 bone-in loin chops
- 1 cup natural pistachio nuts, shelled, ground to a powder
- Olive oil

Ground pistachio nuts make a fine and crispy coating for these succulent tasting pork chops. This is a perfect company dish.

Preheat the oven to 350°F.

Lightly beat the eggs in a bowl with the rosemary, salt, and a grinding of black pepper.

Coat each chop in the pistachio dust and set aside.

Heat the olive oil in a stovetop-to-oven sauté pan large enough to hold the chops without crowding them.

Brown the chops quickly on both sides, then slide the pan into a 350°F oven, and bake them until the internal temperature reaches 160°F. Serve hot.

Sautéed broccoli rape or mushrooms are nice with the chops.

Serves 4

❖ CHEF'S SECRET: Do not be in a hurry to brown pork chops; allow them to cook sufficiently on one side before flipping them over. They are ready to turn when the outer edges begin to brown.

Pollo in Salsa Agrodolce
Sweet-and-Sour Chicken and Eggplant

What I like about this dish, besides how fast it goes together, is the marriage of leeks and eggplant, a sensational taste of bitter and sweet, or what Italians call agrodolce. *It is the perfect foil for the chicken, which without cleverly used ingredients, would be just chicken.*

Heat the olive oil in a sauté pan set over medium heat; add the leeks and eggplant and cook until the leeks are very soft and creamy and the eggplant begins to brown. Transfer the vegetables to a dish.

Season the chicken strips well with salt and pepper. Brown them in the same pan over medium-high heat, adding more oil, if necessary.

Return the leeks and eggplant to the pan, along with the tomatoes. Reduce the heat to low, cover, and cook for about 8 minutes, or until the chicken is fork-tender.

Serves 4

- ¼ cup olive oil
- 1 large leek, root end and top trimmed and discarded, well-washed, sliced crosswise into thin rings
- 1 small eggplant, peeled and diced
- 1 pound boneless chicken breasts, cut into ½-inch-wide strips
- *Salt to taste*
- *Freshly ground black*
- 3 large plum tomatoes, peeled, seeded, and diced

❖ CHEF'S SECRET: Small-size eggplants have fewer seeds and are less bitter than their larger relatives so there is no need to "sweat" them with salt to remove the bitter juices.

Pollo alla Diavolo
Devilish Chicken

- One 3½- to 4-pound free-range, organic chicken, butterflied
- ¼ cup olive oil
  Fine sea salt
  Freshly ground black pepper
- Cayenne pepper or dried hot red pepper flakes
- 1 cup dry white wine
- Lemon wedges

Pollo alla Diavola *means devilish chicken and gets its name from the fact that* peperoncini, *hot red pepper flakes, are used "a piacere," or to your liking. I use cayenne because the dried pepper flakes tend to burn and fall off during cooking.*

The real success of this dish is based on the quality of the bird. In Tuscany, where this dish is very popular, that means free-range chicken, which has been fed natural grains and treated humanely. The best way to cook the chicken is to butterfly it and place it "alla griglia," on a hot grill. This method allows for even cooking. The results are finger-licking good!

Place the chicken on a plastic cutting board breast side down. With poultry shears or a boning knife, cut along one side of the backbone, then cut down the other side of the backbone. Remove and discard the bone or save for stock.

Open out the chicken and flatten it by pressing down with your hands, or use a meat pounder. Rub the chicken all over with the olive oil, then season it with salt, pepper, and cayenne. Place the chicken in a dish, cover, and marinate it for several hours; this step can be done the day before.

When you are ready to cook, fire up the grill, and when the coals are white, or a gas grill temperature reaches 500°F, place the chicken on the grill breast side down and cook, turning frequently, and keeping the fire under control so as not to burn the chicken.

Halfway into the grilling, about 10 minutes, start basting the chicken with the wine and continue basting every 10 minutes. The chicken is cooked when a meat thermometer inserted into the thighbone registers between 175° and 180°F.

Transfer the chicken to a cutting board, and cut it into serving pieces. Serve hot with a squirt of lemon juice. Use your fingers, not a fork, to eat it, and keep a glass of water at the ready, just in case the devil gets to you!

Serves 4

Pollo al Limone ed Erbe

Roast Chicken with Lemon and Herbs

- 3 large lemons
- 1 tablespoon dried oregano
- ¼ cup fresh minced flat-leaf parsley
- 1 tablespoon extra-virgin olive oil
  Fine sea salt
  Freshly ground black pepper
- 1 cut up 3½-pound chicken, preferably free-range, organic

Intense flavor happens, like the tangy lemon taste of juicy roasted chicken. This dish is reminiscent of the Amalfi coast, where sunny lemons, fruity olive oil, and fragrant fresh herbs are the heroes of Italian cooking. Look for free-range, organic chicken when making this or other dishes calling for poultry. The flavor and quality is worth the extra cost.

Combine the zest and juice of 2 lemons in a large shallow glass dish. Stir in the oregano, parsley, olive oil, salt, and pepper. Set aside.

Toss the chicken in the marinade. Cover and refrigerate for at least 1 hour or overnight.

Preheat the oven to 350°F.

Transfer the chicken pieces to a lightly oiled roasting pan. Place them in the preheated oven and roast until an instant-read thermometer inserted into the thickest part of the chicken registers 165°F, 35 to 45 minutes depending on your oven. Transfer the chicken to a serving dish. Cut the remaining lemon into wedges and arrange around the chicken.

Serves 6

❖ CHEF'S SECRET: Room-temperature citrus, such as lemons, will yield more juice if rolled under your hands on a countertop before cutting.

Big Five
FISH

Cappesante e Pomodori Fritti

SCALLOPS AND FRIED TOMATOES

Ippoglosso al Forno con Scalogno e Finocchio

OVEN-POACHED HALIBUT WITH SHALLOT AND FENNEL

Passerino Ripieno

STUFFED FLOUNDER WITH SPINACH AND CARROTS

Gamberi Fritti

FRIED SHRIMP

Tonno alle Erbe

TUNA WITH HERBS

Salmone alla Griglia con Cipolle Rosse

GRILLED SAMON WITH RED ONIONS

Fish Tales

My exuberant seafaring friend, Mario Cocco, is Sardinian, so it stands to reason that he knows fish. And just how much he knows was made very apparent when I visited him in the port city of Cagliari where we feasted on roasted eels, one of the specialties of the island. First we sought out the best fishmonger, then we looked at dozens of slithering specimens before he made his meticulous purchase of the plumpest ones. In the kitchen, Mario brushed the tender flesh with olive oil, wrapped them in fragrant myrtle leaves, and put them on a wood fired grill. When they came off the fire with crackling skin, we savored every morsel.

When he visited me in New England, I reciprocated and took him out for lobster. I watched in amazement as he dissected everything like a skilled surgeon, ate everything including the cartilage, and even sucked out the last savory juices of the legs, for which I have no patience. When the server came to take away the clean-as-a-whistle empty lobster bodies, Mario put out his hand like a traffic cop and asked for a bag to take them with him! "We will make the perfect *sugo*," he happily cried!

I have learned a lot about fish from Mario. Freshness and local, these are defining culinary words for Italian cooks. They can tell you where the fish came from, and how to cook it. They know how to scale, de-bone, fillet, and serve it, too. Nothing will be wasted, including head and tail, which will be tossed into a soup pot and turned into a savory fish stock. No heavy sauce will blanket the delicate taste; instead a squirt of lemon juice, a drizzle of olive oil, a few fresh herbs, and a dusting of sea salt will complement its flavor. No dressed down, plastic-wrapped supermarket version of fish will do. Order it in Italy in a restaurant and it will arrive beautifully presented on your plate in tact, head and tail. It is the perfect example of the statement that I made in the introduction to this book about cooking with choice ingredients: less is more.

That is the definition of true Italian soul food for me, and I envy the kind of connection that Italians have for raw ingredients, always respecting their inherent characteristics. Maybe another way to look at it is to call it being mindful, like Mario.

FIVE FISH TIPS

1) The nose knows. Fresh fish does not smell, well, fishy, it smells sweet. So if you detect a whiff of ammonia, that is bad fish.

2) The eyes have it. Fresh fish is plump-looking with no sunken eyes. The skin is shiny and the gills are moist.

3) When purchasing fish or seafood, ask the fishmonger to bag it with ice to keep it cold until you get home.

4) To prevent fish from sticking when browning, get the pan good and hot before adding the fish.

5) Do not overcook fish. It is done when it flakes easily.

Cappesante e Pomodori Fritti

Scallops and Fried Tomatoes

- Sixteen large diver or day boat sea scallops
  Fine sea salt
  Freshly ground black pepper
- 1 cup stone-ground cornmeal
- 2 large beefsteak tomatoes, thickly cut into 4 round slices
- ¾ stick (6 tablespoons) unsalted butter
- ½ cup dry white wine

Beware when purchasing scallops, the best ones are diver or day boat scallops. Diver scallops are collected by hand by divers and they are the largest size—perfect for grilling. Day boat scallops are those that are harvested in a day rather than the traditional method of dredging for up to ten days at sea. Do not buy scallops that are water injected. You will pay for unnecessary weight due to the water, and water-injected scallops will never brown.

Dry the scallops on paper towels. Transfer the scallops to a dish and sprinkle with salt and pepper. Set aside.

Season the cornmeal with salt and pepper. Place it on a plate, and coat each tomato slice on both sides with the mixture.

In a large sauté pan, melt 2 tablespoons of the butter over medium-high heat. Brown the tomato slices on both sides until nice and crusty. Transfer them to a dish and keep them warm.

Wipe out the sauté pan. Melt 1 tablespoon of the remaining butter in the pan, and increase the heat to high. Sear the scallops on each side for about 2 minutes, or until they are nicely browned. Add the remaining butter, gently toss the scallops in the butter, and cook about 3 minutes, turning the scallops frequently. Pour in the wine, and cook for about 2 minutes, scraping up the bits from the bottom of the pan.

Stack 2 tomato slices in the center of each of 4 plates. Place 4 scallops on top of the tomato slices, and spoon some of the pan juices over them. Serve hot.

Serves 4

❖ CHEF'S SECRET: Stone-ground cornmeal contains the hull and the germ, making it a healthier choice than regular processed cornmeal. Once opened, store it in containers in the refrigerator to keep the oils present in cornmeal fresh and to prevent it from turning rancid.

Ippoglosso al Forno con Scalogno e Finocchio
Oven-poached Halibut with Shallot and Fennel

- 4 halibut steaks (about 2 pounds total)
- 1¼ cups dry white wine
- 2 large shallots, minced
- 1 small fennel bulb, trimmed and coarsely chopped
- 1 cup diced cherry tomatoes
- *Fine sea salt*
- *Freshly ground black pepper*

Halibut is a delicate flatfish that is just right for poaching, which means cooking it in some type of liquid that is just below the boiling point. For this preparation, I like white wine, but chicken stock or vegetable stock are good alternatives.

Preheat the oven to 325°F.

Place the halibut in a 13 × 9-inch baking dish.

Combine the wine, shallots, fennel, tomatoes, and salt and pepper in a bowl.

Pour the vegetable mixture over the fish. Bake the halibut for 20 to 25 minutes, or until the fish is opaque and is easily flaked with a fork.

Serve with some of the pan juices drizzled over the fish.

Serves 4

Scallops and Fried Tomatoes (p. 84)

This delicious Cauliflower Salad (p. 112) is a good starter for . . .

Grilled Salmon with Red Onions (p. 90)

Cheesy Stuffed Meatballs (p. 70)

Radicchio, Ricotta Salata, and Dried Apricots (p. 117)

Just five ingredients—pasta, eggs, pecorino, pancetta, and freshly ground black pepper—are all you need to make . . .

. . . the classic Coal Miners'-Style Spaghetti (p. 48)

Grilled Mortadella and
Fontina Cheese Panini (p. 16)

Passerino Ripieno
Stuffed Flounder with
Spinach and Carrots

Flounder is a mild flatfish that is perfect for stuffing. If you cannot find it, use sole or cod fillet instead.

Preheat the oven to 400°F.

Cook the spinach, covered, without any additional water, just until the leaves wilt. Drain and squeeze dry. Coarsely chop the spinach and place it in a bowl. Cook the carrots with the ginger in 2 tablespoons of the butter until the carrots begin to wilt. Transfer them to the bowl with the spinach. Season to taste with salt and pepper.

Divide and spread the spinach-carrot mixture on top of the fish. Starting at the short end, roll each fillet up like a jelly roll.

Brush a casserole dish with 1 tablespoon of the remaining butter. Add the fillets, and drizzle the tops with the remaining 2 tablespoons butter.

Bake the flounder for 20 to 25 minutes, or until the fish turns white and is easily flaked with a fork. Serve hot.

Serves 4

- 1 pound fresh spinach, well washed
- 1 medium carrot, peeled and grated
- 1 tablespoon fresh ginger grated
  Fine sea salt
  Freshly ground black pepper
- 5 tablespoons unsalted butter, melted
- 4 flounder fillets, (about 5 to 6 ounces each)

Gamberi Fritti
Fried Shrimp

- ½ cup all-purpose flour
- *Fine sea salt*
- *Freshly ground black pepper*
- 2 pounds large raw shrimp, (26 to 40 count), shelled and deveined
- ¼ cup minced flat-leaf parsley
- 1 stick (8 tablespoons) unsalted butter
- 2 large eggs, lightly beaten

Today, most shrimp are farm raised, so if you are lucky enough to find fresh Gulf shrimp, these will taste even better. Shrimp are cooked when they turn pink and the tail begins to curl; be careful not to overcook them, or their texture will turn rubbery.

Combine the flour, salt, and pepper in a paper bag. Add the shrimp a few at a time and shake to coat them evenly in the seasoned flour.

Melt the butter in a large sauté pan placed over medium heat.

Coat each shrimp in the beaten egg.

Place the shrimp and parsley in the pan and sauté until golden brown. Serve hot.

Serves 4

> ❖ CHEF'S SECRET: Save the shells. Throw them in a pot with sliced lemons, a bay leaf, celery tops, and a carrot and cover with water. Add salt and pepper to taste. Bring to a boil and cook for 30 minutes. Strain out the broth and save for use in casseroles and fish soups.

Tonno alle Erbe

Tuna with Herbs

While fish has become prohibitively expensive in Italy, it remains a very popular item in the markets and on most restaurant menus.

Tuna, swordfish, and salmon are particularly good choices for this easy preparation, and it is one that you can get ready the night before. A hot cast-iron skillet cooks the fish best; if you do not have one, use a frying or sauté pan, or alternatively cook the fish on a hot grill.

Mince the garlic and thyme together and spread it in the bottom of a glass casserole dish, large enough to hold the fish in a single layer. Place the fish on top and turn to coat on both sides with the herbs and garlic. Marinate the fish, covered in plastic wrap, for 2 hours, turning the pieces occasionally.

Heat the oil in a cast-iron skillet until very hot. Place the fish in the pan and sear over high heat about 2½ minutes on each side.

Sprinkle the fresh basil on top, and serve immediately.

Serves 4

- 1 large garlic clove, peeled
- 4 sprigs fresh thyme, leaves picked
- 3 tablespoons extra-virgin olive oil
  ½ teaspoon fine sea salt
  Freshly ground black pepper
- 1¼ pounds tuna steak, cut into 4 pieces
- 8 fresh basil leaves, shredded

Salmone alla Griglia con Cipolle Rosse

Grilled Salmon with Red Onions

- 2 tablespoons olive oil
- 1 large red onion, peeled, halved, and thickly sliced
  Salt
  Freshly ground black pepper
- 4 salmon steaks, weighing about 6 ounces each
- 2 large oranges, each cut in half; each half cut into 2 wedges

Study the Italian food pyramid, and what you will find is that fish and vegetables make up the bulk of the diet. Because Italy is a peninsula, it stands to reason that fish dishes are popular. Remember this rule when cooking any fish: allow about 10 minutes cooking time per inch of thickness. Now fire up the grill for salmon with grilled onions!

Spray the grill grate with olive oil grilling spray. Preheat a gas or charcoal grill to medium-high heat.

Spread 2 tablespoons of olive oil on ½ of a large sheet of aluminum foil. Add the onions and coat them in the oil. Season with salt and pepper. Fold the other half of aluminum foil over the onions and seal the edges. Place the onion package on the grill.

Place the salmon on the grill along with the orange wedges. Lightly brush the salmon and the orange wedges with olive oil.

Close the grill top and cook for 5 to 7 minutes. Turn once. Turn the onion package once.

The salmon should have nice grill marks, and be moist and pink in the middle.

Transfer the salmon to a platter along with the oranges. Open the aluminum foil and spread the onions over the salmon. Season with salt and pepper and serve. Squeeze the orange juice over the salmon.

Serves 4

Big Five
VEGETABLES

Rapini con Olive
BROCCOLI RAPE WITH OLIVES

Patate in Casseruola
POTATO CASSEROLE

Melanzane Gratinate con Fontina
BAKED EGGPLANT WITH FONTINA

Finocchio in Padella
BRAISED FENNEL

Peperonata
MIXED SWEET PEPPER CASSEROLE

Piselli e Uova
PEAS AND EGGS

Tortina di Funghi e Spinaci e Formaggio
MUSHROOM, SPINACH, AND CHEESE TART

Zucchine Secche
DRIED ZUCCHINI CHIPS

Cipolline Caramellate
CARAMELIZED ONIONS

Zucchine all'arrabiata
HOT AND SPICY ZUCCHINI COINS

Love Me Tender

I love January. Holidays are but a memory, old man winter has settled in for a while, and the new vegetable seed catalogs are stacked high on my kitchen counter. I know how I am getting through the dreary months ahead—planning out my vegetable garden. I am so happy when vegetables are for the taking right out of my garden, it is one of the things as a cook that I look forward to. I can munch to my heart's content on crunchy lettuce, candy-sweet tomatoes, and crisp cucumbers. Even prolific zucchini wins me over as I concoct as many recipes as my family will tolerate.

Vegetables don't ask much from a cook, just a little know-how on treating them properly for maximum flavor. Choosing them in season is key, as well as using them as quickly as possible and subjecting them to minimum cooking, which will preserve their flavor, texture, visual appeal, and nutritional value. Less is more when it comes to cooking time. Vegetables should retain their shape, color, and be tender but not mushy. I have adapted many cooking methods for them, including a quick sauté, steaming, grilling, and my favorite—roasting, which caramelizes the natural sugars and concentrates the flavor.

Come winter and I am like Sherlock Holmes, searching desperately for produce as close to the same quality as that of my garden. I know the pickings will be slim, and I read each label to see how far away from home winter vegetables have traveled. Root vegetables are my mainstay, carrying me through to the first warm days of spring, and the promise of a new garden season in full swing again.

FIVE VEGETABLE TIPS

1) Vegetables need proper storage. Mushrooms, green beans, peppers, asparagus, and broccoli should not be stored in plastic bags as these give off moisture that can make vegetables slimy. Keep them in paper bags, or wrapped in paper towels, and refrigerated.

2) Potatoes, garlic, and onions should be stored in a cool, dark place to avoid sprouting.

3) Buy vegetables in season, and use them within 3 days of purchase to preserve their freshness and nutritional value.

4) When boiling vegetables such as green beans or broccoli, do not cover the pot; this will allow acids to escape and prevent green vegetables from turning gray.

5) Never refrigerate tomatoes or avocados, it will ruin their flavor. Keep them at room temperature.

Rapini Con Olive

Broccoli Rape with Olives

- 1 bunch broccoli rape
- 2 tablespoons extra-virgin olive oil
- 1 tablespoon dried hot red pepper flakes
- 2 garlic cloves, minced
- 8 oil-cured Gaeta or black olives, pitted and coarsely chopped
  Fine sea salt
  Freshly ground black pepper

Broccoli rape, also called rapini or broccoli raab, is a slightly bitter vegetable that is related to turnips. It has been a favorite with Italians since ancient times and is cultivated widely in the Mediterranean. Mixed with olives, it is a sturdy side dish for beef. Other clever uses for it are as a topping for pizza or as a sauce for pasta.

Trim the stems of the broccoli rape, wash and drain the rape, and coarsely chop. Set it aside.

Heat the olive oil in a sauté pan over medium heat, stir in the broccoli rape, and cook for about 2 minutes. Stir in the pepper flakes and garlic, cover the pan, and cook for about 5 minutes over medium heat, or until a small knife is easily inserted into a stem. Uncover the pan, and stir in the olives. Season to taste with salt and pepper. Serve hot.

Serves 4

❖ CHEF'S SECRET: Never buy broccoli or broccoli rape showing any yellow florets; that is a sign of old produce.

Patate in Casseruola
Potato Casserole

This potato casserole in the style of northern Italy is best made with red-skinned, new, or small white potatoes. These are low in starch and hold up well in baking. Serve this casseruola as a side to baked fish, chops, or roasted meats.

Preheat the oven to 400°F.

Brush a 12×9-inch casserole dish or 12-inch cast-iron skillet with 1 tablespoon of the melted butter.

Layer the potatoes in the casserole dish, and pour the remaining melted butter over them.

Whisk the egg, milk, nutmeg, and salt and pepper together in a bowl. Pour evenly over the potatoes.

Bake the casserole, uncovered, for 40 to 45 minutes, or until the top is browned, and a knife is easily inserted into the potatoes. Serve hot.

Serves 4 to 6

- ½ stick (4 tablespoons) unsalted butter, melted
- 2 pounds red-skin potatoes, peeled and thinly sliced
- 1 large egg, lightly beaten
- 1½ cups whole milk
- ½ teaspoon freshly grated nutmeg
- *Fine sea salt*
- *Freshly ground black pepper*

Melanzane Gratinate con Fontina

Baked Eggplant with Fontina

- 4 small eggplant
- 2 garlic cloves
- 5 fresh basil leaves
  Fine sea salt
  Freshly ground black pepper
- ⅔ cup extra-virgin olive oil
- ½ pound Italian fontina cheese, cut into small pieces

Forget messy frying when cooking eggplant; creamy fontina cheese makes this baked eggplant casserole elegant and a nice change from the more common eggplant parm. It's healthier, too!

Preheat the oven to 375°F.

Cut the stems from the eggplant and discard. Cut the eggplant lengthwise in half.

Make small crisscross cuts that are about ½-inch deep in each cut side.

Mince the garlic with the basil, and place in a small bowl. Season with salt and pepper and 1 tablespoon of the olive oil. Set aside.

Insert the cheese into the cuts of the eggplant. Spread the garlic mixture over the cuts.

Place the eggplant in a large baking dish in a single layer, or use two smaller baking dishes. Drizzle the eggplant with the olive oil. Bake for 25 to 30 minutes, or until the eggplant are nicely browned and the cheese is bubbly.

Serves 4

❖ CHEF'S SECRET: Only buy as much cheese for cooking or eating as can be used in a relatively short period of time. Italian fontina comes from the Val d'Aosta region in Italy and is recognized by its reddish brown rind. Do not confuse it with Danish fontina, a harder cheese with an orange red rind.

Finocchio in Padella
Braised Fennel

Feathery anise-flavored fennel is affectionately called finocchio *in Italy. Fennel, a member of the parsley family, was a symbol of flattery in literature and folklore. Flattery will get you everything when you serve this delicious side dish with fish.*

Cut each bulb lengthwise in half and then into quarters, leaving the core attached to keep the layers together.

Melt the butter in a sauté pan large enough to hold the fennel in one layer. When the butter is hot, add the fennel quarters and cook, without turning, for 5 minutes. Turn the fennel over, lower the heat, and pour in the cream along the edge of the pan. Cover the pan and cook the fennel over low heat until it is knife-tender and almost all the cream has evaporated.

Season to taste with salt and pepper. Transfer the fennel to a serving dish, sprinkle the cheese over the slices, and serve.

Serves 8

- 3 large fennel bulbs, white part only, fronds and stalks and root end trimmed
- ¾ stick (6 tablespoons) unsalted butter
- ⅔ cup heavy cream
  Fine sea salt
- ½ cup grated Parmigiano-Reggiano cheese

Peperonata

Mixed Sweet Pepper Casserole

- 3 red sweet bell peppers
- 3 yellow sweet bell peppers
- 1 pound small white onions
- ½ cup extra-virgin olive oil
- 4 large plum tomatoes, seeded and quartered

Fine sea salt

Peperonata is a colorful casserole that has its origins in the south of Italy where the climate is just right for growing peperoni, *peppers. Juicy and sweet, this dish combines red and yellow peppers with small boiling onions and fresh tomatoes. A great summertime treat!*

Use a preheated outdoor grill to char the peppers, or preheat the broiler and char the peppers on a broiler pan, 3 inches away from the broiler element. Turn the peppers occasionally until the skin is blackened on all sides.

Let the peppers cool in a paper bag. When the peppers are cool enough to handle, remove the outer skins and core, and wipe out the seeds with paper towels.

Cut the peppers into ½-inch-wide strips. Set aside.

Put the onions in a small pot, and add enough water to cover. Bring to a boil and cook the onions for 5 minutes. Drain the onions and set aside.

Heat the olive oil in a sauté pan over medium heat. Add the pepper strips and cook for 3 or 4 minutes. Add the onions and tomatoes. Season them to taste with salt, and cook the mixture until it begins to thicken. Serve hot as a side dish with chicken, fish, or pork.

Serves 6

❖ CHEF'S SECRET: Never rinse roasted peppers to remove the seeds; all the flavorful juices will be washed away. Use paper towels instead to wipe away the seeds.

Piselli e Uova

Peas and Eggs

Peas and eggs. What's so special about that? You'll see.

Heat the olive oil in an 8-inch nonstick skillet over low heat. Stir in the pancetta and cook for 5 minutes or until the pancetta renders its fat and begins to crisp. Add the peas, salt, and pepper. Simmer, uncovered, for 2 minutes. With a wooden spoon, spread the peas evenly in the base of the skillet. Crack the eggs carefully over the top of the peas. Cover and cook over medium-low heat for 4 to 6 minutes. The eggs should look poached with a set center yolk and firm egg white.

Serve hot accompanied with the bread slices.

Serves 4

- 3 tablespoons extra-virgin olive oil
- ¼ pound diced pancetta
- 2 cups fresh or frozen peas
  Fine sea salt
  Freshly ground black pepper
- 4 large eggs, at room tempearature
- 4 thick slices semolina or sourdough-type bread

❖ CHEF'S SECRET: Organic eggs have superior flavor, are fresher, and are higher in omega 3.

Tortina di Funghi Spinaci e Formaggio

Mushroom, Spinach, and Cheese Tart

- One 10-ounce box frozen spinach, defrosted and squeezed dry
- 2 tablespoons fresh thyme leaves, minced
- 1½ cups fresh mozzarella cheese, cut into bits
  Salt
  Freshly ground black pepper
- 3 tablespoons extra-virgin olive oil
- 4 large portobello mushrooms, at least 4 inches in diameter stems removed, caps wiped clean with a damp paper towel

Portobello are cultivated mushrooms that are the big brothers of the simple button mushroom. They are popular both marinated and grilled, but stuff their large caps, and they become the "crust" for this spinach and cheese "tart."

Preheat oven to 350°F.

Chop the spinach coarsely and place it in a bowl. Stir in the thyme leaves and half of the cheese. Add salt and pepper to taste. Set aside.

Heat 2 tablespoons of the olive oil in a 12½-inch ovenproof sauté pan over medium heat.

Add the mushrooms, cap sides down, and cook them for 2 or 3 minutes, covered. Remove the pan from the heat, and fill each mushroom cap with some of the spinach and cheese mixture, dividing it equally among the mushroom caps. Sprinkle the remaining cheese evenly over the filling. Drizzle the caps with the remaining 1 tablespoon of oil.

Cover the pan, place it in the preheated oven, and bake the mushrooms for 25 to 30 minutes. Uncover the pan and continue baking until the filling is hot and the cheese is bubbly. Serve hot.

Serves 4

❖ CHEF'S SECRET: Cut each baked cap into quarters and serve as part of an antipasto.

Zucchine Secche

Dried Zucchini Chips

This recipe was hatched from desperation when my zucchini plants, which seemed to have nine lives (and then some), conquered my garden. Dried zucchini chips are a great way to use up that army of green and makes the best healthful snack. Pick the zucchini when they are about six inches long. Take care to dry the slices well, until they are as crisp as potato chips, or they will mold. I use a dehydrator, but drying them in the oven works, too. Happy munching!

Combine the oregano, salt, cayenne, and celery salt in a paper bag. Add the zucchini rounds in batches and shake to coat well.

Place the slices on the racks of a dehydrator and dry them according to the manufacturer's directions until the slices are crisp like potato chips. Or place the slices on wire racks atop baking sheets, and dry them in a 175°F oven, rotating the sheets occasionally. Drying time could be anywhere from 1 to 2 days.

Transfer the chips to clean glass jars. Cap the jars and store them in a cool, dark place.

Eat them like potato chips!

Makes approximately 1½ cups,
will vary with size of zucchini

- 1 tablespoon dried oregano
  1½ teaspoons coarse sea salt
- ¼ teaspoon ground cayenne pepper
- 1 teaspoon celery salt
- 6 small zucchini, washed, dried, and thinly sliced into ¼-inch-thick rounds

Cipolline Caramellate

Caramelized Onions

- 1 pound unpeeled small cippoline or white boiling onions
  2 teaspoons fine sea salt
- ¼ pound pancetta, diced
- 1 teaspoon olive oil
- ½ cup sweet Marsala wine
- ¼ cup honey

I adore caramelized onions! Their sweet taste is a perfect contrast for game meats, poultry, or even fish. I confess, I enjoy them all by themselves! Use cippoline onions if you can find them, or small boiling onions.

Place the onions in a 2-quart saucepan. Cover with water and add the salt. Cover and bring to a boil. Reduce the heat to medium, and cook the onions just until a knife is easily inserted into them. Drain the onions in a colander. When they are cool enough to handle, slip off and discard the skins. Set the onions aside.

Cook the pancetta over medium heat with the olive oil in a sauté pan. When the pancetta is soft, add the onions and the wine and cook until the wine has almost evaporated. As soon as the wine has evaporated, stir in the honey. Cook slowly over medium-low heat, turning the onions occasionally, until they are nicely glazed. Transfer the onions to a bowl, and serve them warm as an accompaniment to meats and poultry.

Serves 4

❖ CHEF'S SECRET: Store onions in a cool, dark, but not cold, spot. This will prevent them from sprouting and spoiling.

Zucchine all'arrabiata

Hot and Spicy Zucchini Coins

Test your tastebuds with tender, small-size zucchini coins sautéed in olive oil and mixed with just a teaspoon of hot red pepper paste. A hot and spicy perfect side dish that can go with anything!

Heat the olive oil over medium-high heat in a medium-size sauté pan, and when the oil begins to shimmer, add the zucchini and stir a few times. Cover the pan, lower the heat to simmer, and cook for 3 to 4 minutes, or just until the zucchini begins to brown.

Stir in the pepper paste or pepper flakes and cook 2 to 3 minutes longer, or just until the zucchini is tender. Stir in the cheese and parsley. Sprinkle with the coarse salt and serve hot.

Serves 4

- 2 tablespoons olive oil
- 4 small zucchini, ends trimmed, cut into ¼-inch round coins
- 1 teaspoon hot red pepper paste or 1 teaspoon dried hot red pepper flakes
- 2 tablespoons minced flat-leaf parsley
- 2 tablespoons grated Pecorino cheese
½ teaspoon coarse sea salt

Big Five
SALADS

Insalata di Barbabietola ed Arance

BEET AND ORANGE SALAD

Insalata di Cavolfiore

CAULIFLOWER SALAD

Insalata di Asparagi e Peperoni Rossi

ASPARAGUS AND RED PEPPER SALAD

Insalata Scarola

ESCAROLE SALAD WITH MUSTARD DRESSING

Insalata di Sedano e Funghi

CELERY AND MUSHROOM SALAD

Insalata di Finocchio Mele e Carote

FENNEL, APPLE, AND CARROT SALAD

Insalata di Radicchio Ricotta Salata e Albicocche

RADICCHIO, RICOTTA SALATA, AND DRIED APRICOT SALAD

Insalata di Spinaci Robiola e Pere

SPINACH, ROBIOLA, AND PEAR SALAD

Getting A-Head (of Lettuce)

Who can't make a salad from scratch? Lots of people. That's why prewashed, prepackaged salad greens are a popular sale item in most grocery stores. All you have to do is open the bag and dump the contents into a salad bowl. Grab your favorite bottled dressing, add some crunchy croutons, and salad is ready! You never have to hold a head of crisp fresh lettuce in your hands or distinguish between Boston bibb, Romaine, or endive.

One of the healthiest foods you can eat is salad and it should be the freshest that it can be! During dreary winter months, most lettuce travels on average more than 1,500 miles to your store. Pickings can be slim but it still is worth buying that head of lettuce instead of a prewashed bag of leaves. Look for lettuces that are locally greenhouse grown, or support your farmers' market. Try to vary salads by mixing greens with fresh fruits like pears, oranges, strawberries, and pomegranate seeds. Use nuts like pine nuts, almonds, or walnuts instead of croutons. This will add interest, stave off boredom, and encourage healthy eating.

FIVE SALAD TIPS

1) Invest in a salad spinner; it refreshes and rehydrates the greens.

2) Even if you buy prewashed greens, wash them again before using to refresh them.

3) The darker the greens the better they are for you.

4) Buy lettuce still attached to its root-ball; this is fresher.

5) Wrap washed leaves in paper towels to absorb excess moisture.

Insalata di Barbabietola ed Arance

Beet and Orange Salad

Beets—red, orange, or striped varieties—pair nicely with orange slices in this easy to make salad that is a perfect accompaniment to the Soppressata Tartlets on page 20. Roasting the beets instead of boiling them retains much of their color and caramelizes their taste so that even people who don't like beets will be more than tempted to give this salad a try!

Preheat the oven to 400°F.

Wrap each beet in aluminium foil and place on a baking sheet. Bake until a small knife easily pierces the beets, about 15 minutes. Cool, unwrap, and peel the beets. Slice them into ¼-inch thick rounds and place them in a rectangular glass pan.

Whisk the olive oil, vinegar, and salt together and pour over the beets. Toss to coat them well. Cover and allow the beets to marinate for several hours or overnight. When ready to serve, toss the beets with the mint and orange segments. Serve on individual salad plates.

Serves 4

- 4 medium-size un-peeled beets, tops discarded
- ⅓ cup extra-virgin olive oil
- 3 tablespoons white balsamic vinegar
  Fine sea salt
- ¼ cup minced mint
- 2 large navel oranges, peeled and cut into segments

Insalata di Cavolfiore
Cauliflower Salad

- 1 small head of yellow, white, or purple cauliflower, leaves and core discarded, and separated into 1-inch florets
- ¼ cup diced scallions
- 1 large garlic clove, minced
- ½ cup extra-virgin olive oil

Salt to taste

- ¼ cup white balsamic vinegar

Cauliflower is one of my favorite vegetables, and now it comes in colors, too—deep yellow, rose, and purple! So why not make a great salad? This one has an agrodolce taste (sweet and sour).

Blanch the cauliflower florets in salted water for 1 minute. Drain and shock in ice water for 3 minutes. Drain and dry the florets. Place them in a salad bowl.

Whisk the olive oil, vinegar, salt, scallions, and garlic together. Pour over cauliflower in bowl and toss well. Allow to marinate for 30–45 minutes at room temperature before serving.

Serves 6

❖ VARIATION: For an even tastier dish, add a ½ cup of raisins in the end and toss.

Insalata di Asparagi e Peperoni Rossi

Asparagus and Red Pepper Salad

This versatile roasted asparagus and sweet red bell pepper salad doubles as a great antipasto when accompanied by slices of prosciutto di Parma, assorted cured olives, and chips of Parmigiano-Reggiano cheese. Put it together early in the day or the day before to allow the flavors to really blend well.

- 4 sweet red bell peppers (about 2 pounds)
- ¼ cup plus 3 tablespoons extra-virgin olive oil
- 2 pounds asparagus, stalks trimmed
- ¼ cup balsamic vinegar
- *Fine sea salt*

Preheat the broiler.

Place the peppers on a broiler pan and broil, 3 inches away from the broiler element, turning, until blackened all over. Transfer the peppers to a dish and allow to cool. Remove the stems, peel away the skin and core, and wipe the seeds out with paper towels. Cut the peppers into ¼-inch-wide strips. Set aside. (Alternatively you can char the peppers on a grill.)

Preheat the oven to 350°F.

Brush a baking sheet with 1½ tablespoons of the olive oil. Place the asparagus on the baking sheet and turn to coat in the oil. Roast for 5 to 7 minutes, or until a knife is easily inserted into the stalk.

Transfer the asparagus to a cutting board, and cut crosswise in half. Arrange the asparagus on a platter with the charred bell pepper strips. Combine the remaining olive oil, the balsamic vinegar, and salt and pour over the salad. Cover the salad and let it marinate at room temperature for several hours before serving.

Serves 8

Insalata Scarola
Escarole Salad with Mustard Dressing

- 1 head escarole, leaves separated, soaked in water, and spun dry
- ½ teaspoon dry English mustard
- ⅓ cup extra-virgin olive oil
- 2 tablespoons freshly squeezed lemon juice, or wine vinegar
- 1 tablespoon sugar
  Fine sea salt
  Freshly ground black pepper

Escarole, scarola, *is a bitter green belonging to the chicory family. As a salad green, it is often passed over in favor of the less interesting and less nutritious iceberg lettuce. There is one important thing I have learned about leafy greens, the darker the color, the better. True, escarole needs care and attention to clean the dirt lurking in its leaves, but several soakings in cold water does the trick. Crunchy escarole leaves are perfect for this salad with a tangy mustard vinaigrette.*

Break the escarole leaves into small pieces and place them in a salad bowl.

Whisk the mustard, olive oil, lemon juice or vinegar, and sugar and salt and pepper to taste until well blended. Pour the dressing over the leaves, and toss well to coat.

Serves 4

Insalata di Sedano e Funghi
Celery and Mushroom Salad

One of my favorite things to do in Italy is forage for mushrooms with the locals who know where the best are lurking. And even though I cannot get the same mushrooms at home, delicate types like oyster mushrooms are perfect for this popular celery and mushroom salad.

Gently toss the celery and mushrooms in a bowl; add the lemon juice and olive oil. Toss again. Add salt and pepper to taste. Transfer the salad to a platter, and sprinkle the shavings of cheese over the top. Serve at room temperature.

Serves 4

- 4 celery ribs, sliced paper-thin
- ½ pound oyster mushrooms, stems trimmed, and caps thinly sliced
- Juice of 1 large lemon or lime
- Extra-virgin olive oil
  Coarse sea salt
  Freshly ground black pepper
- Asiago cheese, shaved

Insalata di Finocchio Mele e Carote

Fennel, Apple, and Carrot Salad

- Juice of 2 large limes
- 4 tablespoons honey
- 1 small fennel bulb, shaved
- 1 Golden Delicious apple, cored, peeled, halved, and thinly sliced
- 2 large carrots, peeled and shaved
- *Fine sea salt*

Use a vegetable peeler or a mandoline to make paper-thin shavings of fennel and carrots for this colorful fall salad with a warm honey dressing.

Combine the lime juice and honey in a small saucepan over low heat and warm and stir until well combined.

Toss the fennel, apple, and carrots together in a salad bowl.

Drizzle the honey dressing over the salad; toss well, salt to taste, and serve immediately.

Serves 4

Insalata di Radicchio Ricotta Salata e Albicocche

Radicchio, Ricotta Salata, and Dried Apricot Salad

It took awhile, but radicchio, chubby ruby red balls of chicory with white veining, has become the darling of the salad bowl. Combined with crumbled ricotta salata cheese and dried apricots, it makes a supertasting and out of the ordinary salad.

Whisk the olive oil, vinegar, and salt to taste in a salad bowl. Add the radicchio and cheese and toss well to coat with the dressing. Sprinkle the apricots over the top, and serve.

Serves 4

- ¼ cup extra-virgin olive oil
- 2 tablespoons rice wine vinegar
  Fine sea salt
- 1 small head radicchio, washed, dried, and torn into bite-size pieces
- ¼ pound ricotta salata cheese, crumbled
- 6 dried apricots, cut into small pieces

Insalata di Spinaci Robiola e Pere

Spinach, Robiola, and Pear Salad

- 4 cups fresh spinach, stemmed, washed, and dried
- 2 large ripe Anjou pears, peeled, cored, and cut into ¼-inch-thick slices
- ¼ pound Robiola cheese, cut into bits
- ⅓ cup extra-virgin olive oil
- 2 tablespoons honey, warmed

Fine sea salt

Robiola cheese is a creamy combination of cow's, sheep's, or goat's milk that is cooked and aged for twenty days. It is thought to have originated in Lombardia. Rich and smooth with the texture of brie, it is exquisite enjoyed on its own, but add it to this spinach and pear salad, and prepare to delight your taste buds.

Place the spinach leaves in a salad bowl. Add the pear slices and cheese.

In a separate bowl whisk together the olive oil, honey, and salt to taste. Pour the dressing over the salad and mix gently. Serve immediately.

Serves 4

❖ CHEF'S SECRET: Keep sliced pears in lemon juice to prevent discoloring when preparing ahead.

Pavia's Poached Egg Soup (p. 31)

Baked in a rectangle on parchment or in an irregular shape (opposite) that you might encounter somewhere in Italy . . .

. . . this delicious Prosciutto and Pine Nut Pizza (p. 19) is an easy and delicious lunch or dinner when paired with a crisp green salad.

Five-ingredient dishes are versatile. The Cauliflower Salad (p. 112) that made such a good starter for salmon is also a winner when paired with . . .

. . . Pistachio-Dusted Pork Chops (p. 74)

Almond Crisps (p. 124)

These delicious Chocolate, Hazelnut, and Banana Tartlets (p. 132) start as easy-to-bake tart shells filled with sliced bananas and end up . . .

. . . . as gorgeous banana-topped chocolate treats for dessert.

Big Five
SWEETS

❦

Amaretti Fini
ALMOND CRISPS

Biscotti al Limone
LEMON WAFER COOKIES

Crostata di Marmellata
JAM TART

Torta di Gelato
GELATO PIE

Lingue di Gatto
CATS' TONGUES

La Torta della Mamma
MOM'S SPONGE CAKE

Tortine di Gianduja e Banana
CHOCOLATE, HAZELNUT, AND
BANANA TARTLETS

Meringhe
PUFFY MERINGUES

*Mele al Forno con le Noci
e Marmellata*
BAKED APPLES WITH NUTS
AND MARMALADE

Nocciolata
NUTTY SQUARES

Panna Cotta con Vaniglia
BUTTERMILK PANNA COTTA
WITH VANILLA

*Pere al Pepe Nero
e Vaniglia*
POACHED PEARS WITH BLACK
PEPPERCORNS AND VANILLA

Sweet Bites

How do they do it? Reserve their sweet tooth for special occasions? It must be sheer willpower that drives the Italian restraint for daily sugar highs, replacing their cravings with fruits in season.

Italians do not bake at home. Why should they when the streets of Italy are lined with *pasticerri* (pastry shops) selling gorgeous-looking cakes, tarts, and biscotti? Italians are more likely to purchase sweets to bring to someone as a gift or to show hospitality when entertaining at home. I have been in many pastry shops all over the "boot," and have succumbed to sweet temptations from cornmeal cookies in the north to crisp cannoli in the south. The best part is watching your order being wrapped so beautifully like a present, with wrapping paper and a bow, even if it is just two biscotti! No paper bags here!

Do Italians crave a favorite sweet? Hands down it has to be gelato. No afternoon *passeggiata*, the daily stroll Italians enjoy, would be complete without a cone or cup in hand! That said, it is fair to say that Italians do in fact eat sweets every day when you consider that what constitutes a typical Italian breakfast is usually biscotti, or *cornetti* (similar to croissants), and a cappuccino, making the perfect start to *la dolce vita*.

FIVE SWEET TIPS

1) When making biscotti, use parchment paper to line the baking sheets. This will eliminate unnecessary cleanup.

2) Partially freeze cakes that need to be frosted; this eliminates having unsightly crumbs in the icing.

3) Make and freeze pies unbaked; when ready to bake, place them, frozen, in a cold oven and bring it up to baking temperature. Continue baking according to the recipe.

4) Use a serrated knife to cut through soft sponge and angel food–type cakes

5) Keep open bags of flour in the refrigerator to keep them fresh.

Amaretti Fini

Almond Crisps

- ¾ cup blanched almonds
- ¾ cup sugar
- 2 tablespoons grated orange zest
- *Pinch of fine sea salt*
- 2 large egg whites, at room temperature
- ¼ teaspoon almond extract

The perfect elegant cookies for tea are these dainty almond crisps delicately scented with orange zest.

Preheat the oven to 350°F.

Line two or more baking sheets with parchment paper and set them aside.

Grind the almonds in a food processor until they are almost the consistency of flour. Transfer the nut flour to a bowl, and stir in the sugar, orange zest, and salt. Set aside.

In a separate bowl beat the whites and almond extract together until soft peaks form. Do not overbeat, or the egg whites will be too dry. They should look soft and shiny and hang from a rubber spatula without falling off.

Fold the whites into the almond mixture with a rubber spatula, folding gently so as not to deflate the batter.

Using a teaspoon, spoon the batter onto the baking sheets, spacing it 1-inch apart. Bake the cookies for 15 minutes, or until the edges are lightly browned.

Remove the baking sheets from the oven, and transfer the parchment-paper sheet with the cookies still on it to a wire cooling rack. Do not attempt to remove the cookies from the paper immediately, or they will crumble. When they are cool, use a butter knife to loosen them from the parchment paper, and cool completely on the wire rack.

Makes 3 dozen

❖ CHEF'S SECRET: Once opened, all nuts should be stored in the refrigerator or freezer to prevent their oils from drying out and becoming rancid.

Citrus zests (orange, lemon, lime, and grapefruit) can be wrapped in small plastic bags and frozen for up to 3 months.

Biscotti al Limone

Lemon Wafer Cookies

- 3 large eggs
- 1 cup sugar
- 2 tablespoons freshly squeezed Meyer lemon juice, or 1 tablespoon each fresh lemon and orange juice
- 1½ cups unbleached, all-purpose flour
- Grated zest of 1 large Meyer lemon, or 1 teaspoon grated lemon zest and 1 teaspoon grated orange zest

Pinch of fine sea salt

These simple lemon wafer cookies need no embellishment. They are a good accompaniment to fresh fruit, ice cream, and sorbet. Sandwich them together with jam or pastry cream for a fancy presentation and a new look. Meyer lemons, a cross between lemons and oranges, provide a more intense flavor. If they are unavailable, use lemon and orange juice in the recipe.

Preheat the oven to 350°F.

Lightly butter two baking sheets or line them with parchment paper. Set them aside.

In a bowl, beat together the eggs, lemon juice, and sugar until pale and thick. Don't rush this process. The eggs should have lots of air beaten into them and fall off the beaters in ribbons. Sprinkle one-third of the flour over the egg mixture and fold it in with a rubber spatula. Gradually fold in the remaining flour and then the salt and lemon zest.

Drop the batter by teaspoonfuls onto the lined baking sheets, spacing them about 1 inch apart. Bake the cookies for about 15 minutes, or until the edges are lightly browned. Let cool on the baking sheets before transferring them to a wire cooling rack.

Makes about 5 dozen

Crostata alla Marmellata
Jam Tart

Company coming? Let them eat crostata *(jam tart)! The dough is easily made by hand or in a food processor. Just remember a few things: measure the flour correctly by lightly sprinkling it into a metal or plastic one-cup dry measure, and use really cold butter to achieve a flaky crust.*

Combine the flour, butter, sugar, and salt in a mixing bowl or in a food processor and mix or pulse until the mixture is coarse looking.

Add the egg yolks and continue mixing or pulsing until a soft, but not sticky, ball of dough forms. If the dough is too sticky, add a bit more flour.

Wrap the dough in wax paper and refrigerate it for a couple of hours, or make the day before.

Preheat the oven to 375°F.

Roll two-thirds of the dough out to fit a lightly buttered 9-inch tart pan. Lay a piece of parchment paper or aluminum foil over the dough and fill it with dried beans or rice. Bake the shell in the preheated oven for 20 minutes. Remove the paper with the beans or rice. Let the tart cool for 5 minutes.

Spread the jam in the tart shell and set it aside.

Roll out the remaining dough into a 9-inch diameter and cut it into ½-inch-wide strips. Place the strips in a lattice pattern over the tart by pinching off excess dough with your fingers or cutting it off with a small knife, and even the edges. Bake the *crostata* for 20 minutes, or until the crust is golden brown.

Place on a wire rack to cool. Cut into wedges to serve.

Makes one 9-inch tart

- 2 cups unbleached, all-purpose flour
- 1 stick (8 tablespoons) cold unsalted butter, cut into bits (plus extra for pan)
- ½ cup sugar
  Pinch of fine sea salt
- 2 egg yolks, lightly beaten
- Apricot or Raspberry Jam

Torta di Gelato

Gelato Pie

- 3 cups stale butter cookies, chocolate cookies, or cake crumbs, toasted, then crumbled
- ¼ cup finely minced nuts such as almonds, walnuts, or pine nuts
- ¾ stick (6 tablespoons) unsalted butter, melted
- 1 pint vanilla ice cream, or a flavor of your choice, softened
- 1 pint chocolate ice cream, or another flavor of your choice, softened

Stale cookies and cake crumbs become the perfect instant "crust" that can be made in minutes for a gelato pie.

Put the crumbs and nuts in a medium bowl and pour the melted butter over them. Mix well with your hands. Reserve ½ cup of the mixture. Pat the remaining mixture evenly in the bottom and halfway up the sides of a 9-inch pie plate.

Spread the vanilla ice cream over the crumbs. Place the pie in the freezer until the ice cream has hardened. Spread the chocolate ice cream over the vanilla. Sprinkle the reserved crumb and nut mixture over the top. Cover the pie and return it to the freezer to harden.

Remove the pie at least 20 minutes prior to serving. When ready to serve, cut into wedges.

Serves 8

❖ CHEF'S SECRET: To soften the ice cream, put it in a microwave for 30 seconds. This will make it easy to spread.

Lingue di Gatto
Cats' Tongues

There are many versions of lingue di gatto, *cats' tongues, but this remains my favorite. It is a very versatile cookie that looks like a ladyfinger or, by a short stretch of the imagination, a tongue. Serve them as is, or frost the tops with a thin glaze of bittersweet chocolate. Or sandwich them together with chocolate and a smidge of jam, or just with jam alone.*

Preheat the oven to 450°F.

Position the oven racks in the center and upper parts of the oven. Line two baking sheets with parchment paper, or lightly butter and flour them. In a bowl, with an electric mixer, beat the butter, sugar, and vanilla until creamy. Gradually beat in the flour, a few spoonfuls at a time.

In a clean bowl, with clean beaters, beat the egg whites until stiff but not dry peaks form. Fold the whites into the butter mixture, taking care not to deflate the whites.

Fill a pastry bag, fitted with a ½-inch plain tip, with the batter and pipe out 3-inch-long cookies on the lined baking sheets, spacing them 1 inch apart.

Bake the cookies for 5 to 7 minutes, rotating the baking sheets once, until they are firm to the touch but still pale and only very lightly browned around the edges. Remove them to wire cooling racks.

Makes about 3½ dozen

- 1¾ sticks (14 tablespoons) unsalted butter, softened
- 1 cup confectioners' sugar, sifted
- 1 tablespoon vanilla extract
- 2 cups unbleached, all-purpose flour, sifted
- 3 large egg whites, at room temperature

La Torta della Mamma

Mom's Sponge Cake

- 5 large eggs, at room temperature, separated
- 1 cup sugar
- 1 cup sifted unbleached all-purpose flour
- 2 tablespoons freshly squeezed lemon or orange juice plus the zest of one orange or lemon
- 1 tablespoon vanilla or almond extract

½ teaspoon fine sea salt

As long as I have been eating cake, the one that holds the most memories for me is my mother's sponge cake (pan di spagna), *made every Saturday afternoon in anticipation of Sunday dinner and drop-in guests. A sponge cake is rightly named; light like a sponge and able to absorb wonderful flavorings and fillings.*

Preheat the oven to 350°F.

Beat the egg yolks in a large bowl with a handheld mixer until thick and lemon colored, about 3 to 5 minutes. Gradually beat in half of the sugar until dissolved. Beat in the flour until well blended. Stir in the lemon or orange juice, vanilla or almond extract, and salt. Stir in the zest. Set aside.

Use a stand mixer or hand mixer with clean beaters and beat the egg whites until foamy. Beat in the remaining sugar, 2 tablespoons at a time, until soft, glossy peaks form. Set aside.

Fold the beaten egg whites and sugar gently into the egg yolk mixture with a wide rubber spatula, taking care not to deflate the whites. Scoop the batter into a 9×3-inch tube pan. Tap the pan on the counter to remove any air pockets and settle the batter so that it is even in the pan.

Bake the cake for 30 to 35 minutes, or until a cake tester inserted in the center of the cake comes out clean, and the cake is evenly browned and springs back when lightly touched in the center. Invert the cake pan over the neck of a wine bottle, or if the pan has prongs, invert it on a wire cooling rack. Cool completely.

Using a butter knife, loosen the cake all around the inside of the pan and around the center tube. Gently shake the cake out.

Enjoy this sponge cake plain, with a dusting of confectioners' sugar over the top, or coated with a thin glaze made with confectioners' sugar and lemon juice.

For a fancy occasion, cut the cake into three layers and fill the layers with sweetened whipped cream and fresh raspberries.

Makes 8 to 10 servings

Tortine di Gianduja e Banana

Chocolate, Hazelnut, and Banana Tartlets

- 1 sheet prepared puff pastry
- 1 cup Nutella
- 8 ounces mascarpone cheese, at room temperature
- 3 tablespoons sugar
- 1 banana, sliced

Nutella, chocolate hazelnut spread, is all the rage in Italy; "Nutellaphiles" eat it by the spoonful right out of the jar. And that may be as good tasting as it gets unless you decide to make these puff pastry tartlets. Nutella, mixed with mascarpone cheese and spread on top of banana slices in ready-made puff pastry is one of the easiest desserts I know.

Preheat the oven to 425°F.

Roll out the sheet of puff pastry onto a clean work surface and into a 12×14-inch rectangle; cut out four 6-inch circles from the rolled dough. Press and line each of the circles into four individual 3-inch tartlet pans with removable bottoms.

Place the tartlet pans on a baking sheet and poke each shell with a fork all over the surface to prevent puffing while baking. Bake the tartlet shells for 7 to 8 minutes, or until they are nicely browned.

Remove the tartlet pans from the oven and allow them to cool completely.

In a medium bowl use a hand mixer to whip the Nutella and mascarpone together with the sugar until well blended.

Place a layer of banana slices in the bottom of each cooled tartlet shell, then spoon the Nutella mixture into the shells. Refrigerate for several hours before serving.

Serves 4

Meringhe

Puffy Meringues

Meringues have few ingredients, but care is needed to make them right. They should have an airy and dry texture, so don't try to make them on a humid day. Serve them with ice cream in a parfait glass for a new twist on an ice cream sundae.

Preheat the oven to 250°F.

Use a stand mixer to beat the whites on medium speed until they are foamy; add the salt and cream of tartar. Increase the speed to high, and whip until medium peaks form; slowly add the sugar, one tablespoon at a time, and continue beating until stiff peaks form. Beat in the extract and vinegar.

Line two baking sheets with parchment paper. Fill a pastry bag, fitted with a star tip, half full with the meringue, and pipe out 1-inch size drops, spacing them one inch apart. Or use two teaspoons to drop about a tablespoon-size amount onto the parchment paper. Refill the bag, and pipe out the remaining meringues.

Bake the meringues for 25 to 30 minutes. Do not open the oven while they are baking. At the end of baking, turn off the oven and allow them to remain in the oven for 1 hour. Remove the baking sheets from the oven and allow the meringues to cool completely before transferring them to a cooling rack.

Makes about 6 dozen

❖ VARIATIONS: Fold nuts, chocolate, dried fruits, toffee, crushed peppermint candy, or other favorites into the meringue after it is beaten to stiff peaks.

- 4 large egg whites, at room temperature
- ¼ teaspoon fine sea salt
- ½ teaspoon cream of tartar
- 1 cup sugar
- 1 teaspoon almond extract
- 1 teaspoon white vinegar

Mele al Forno con Le Noci e Marmellata

Baked Apples with Nuts and Marmalade

- 4 large Cortland apples, cored
- ¼ cup coarsely chopped walnuts
- 3 teaspoons orange marmalade
- 1 tablespoon unsalted butter, cut into 4 pieces
- ½ cup orange juice

Need a healthy dessert in a hurry? Bake apples Italian style by utilizing the microwave. In 8 minutes or less you will have baked apples that are a perfect wintertime treat. Cortland is the best apple to use for this recipe because it holds its shape. To save time, make these before preparing the rest of the meal. Pop them into the microwave while serving dinner and they will be just the right temperature when you are ready to serve them.

Place the apples in each of 4 individual microwave-proof bowls.

In a small bowl, mix together the walnuts and orange marmalade. Using a small spoon, fill the cavity of each apple with some of the mixture. Place a piece of butter on top of each apple. Carefully pour 2 tablespoons of the orange juice in the base of each bowl.

Bake the apples in a microwave on high power for 5 to 8 minutes. The apples should hold their shape but be soft.

Allow the apples to cool for 5 minutes before serving.

Serves 4

Nocciolata

Nutty Squares

In a hurry and need something fast for dessert? Make nocciolata, *rich, shortbread-like squares, chocked full of nuts. Their crunchy texture is a perfect match for ice cream or a fresh fruit salad. Their heartiness satisfies with tea or coffee, and nestled in a pretty tin, they make the perfect gift.*

- ½ pound shelled walnut halves
- ½ pound shelled whole almonds
- 1 pound unsalted butter, melted and cooled
- 5 cups unbleached, all-purpose flour
- 2½ cups sugar

Preheat the oven to 350°F.

Place the nuts on a baking sheet and toast them for 8 to 10 minutes on the middle oven shelf. Watch them carefully; nuts have a sneaky way of over-browning and burning. As soon as they smell fragrant, remove them from the oven. Transfer the nuts to a bowl and allow them to cool. Then coarsely chop them, and set them aside.

Combine the flour and sugar in a large bowl. Pour in the melted butter, and combine the mixture well. Stir in the nuts. The mixture will be stiff; it is best to do this by hand.

Spread and pat the mixture out evenly onto a 17 × 11½-inch non-stick rimmed baking sheet.

Transfer to the oven and bake the nocciolata on the bottom rack for 25 minutes, or until the top and edges are nicely browned.

Cool slightly; then cut into 2-inch squares.

Makes 8 dozen

❖ CHEF'S SECRET: To store these squares for future use Glad Press'n Seal wrap. It really keeps the air out and ice crystals from forming. Wrap the squares in twos; that way you can take out just what you need. Place the wrapped squares in Ziploc bags or in freezer tins, and freeze for up to two months.

Panna Cotta con Vaniglia
Buttermilk Panna Cotta with Vanilla

- ½ cup low-fat buttermilk, at room temperature
- 1 envelope unflavored gelatin
- One 2-inch-long piece vanilla bean
- ¼ cup plus 2 tablespoons sugar
- 2 cups heavy cream

How could something so simple to make taste so good? True to its name, (cooked cream), this dessert is not for the faint of heart dieter. Serve it for a special occasion, or when you just want a treat.

Grease four ½-cup ramekins lightly with butter and set aside.

Pour the buttermilk into a small bowl, sprinkle on the gelatin, and stir to dissolve. Set aside.

With a small knife, split the vanilla bean in half lengthwise and scrape the seeds into a medium saucepan. Off the heat, add the vanilla bean pod, heavy cream, sugar, and half-and-half.

Stir in the buttermilk and gelatin mixture.

Place the pan over medium heat and cook, stirring constantly with a wooden spoon, until the mixture is just under a boil.

Remove the pan from the heat, and remove the vanilla bean pod.

Carefully pour the mixture into the ramekins. Place them on a tray, and cover with plastic wrap. Refrigerate the panna cotta until set, about 5 hours or overnight.

To serve, run a butter knife around the inside edge of the ramekins, or dip the bottom of each one quickly in hot water then invert the panna cotta onto individual dessert plates and serve at once. This is wonderful as is, but it is even better when served with a fresh fruit or rich chocolate sauce.

Serves 4

❖ CHEF'S SECRET: Whipping cream and heavy cream are not the same; whipping cream has stabilizers.

Pere al Pepe Nero e Vaniglia
Poached Pears with Black Peppercorns and Vanilla

Pears paired with cheese are good, but pears poached in white wine with peppercorns and the essence of vanilla bean are even better. They take minutes to prepare. Serve them for breakfast, lunch, or dessert.

In a medium saucepan, combine the wine, sugar, and salt. Bring the mixture to a boil, reduce to a simmer, and cook until the sugar dissolves and a syrup forms.

Slit the vanilla bean lengthwise and, using the tip of a small knife, scrape the seeds into the poaching syrup mixture. Add the vanilla bean pod and the peppercorns. Stir well.

Remove the pear stems and cut the pears in half lengthwise; remove and discard the core and seeds. Cut each pear half into ¼-inch-thick slices. Add the slices to the wine mixture. Increase the heat to low, and poach the pears for 5 minutes. Turn off the heat and allow the pears to cool to room temperature in the pan.

When ready to serve, remove the vanilla bean and transfer the pears and some of the poaching syrup to a decorative serving bowl, or serve in individual goblets.

Serves 4

- 2 cups white wine, such as Pinot Grigio or Soave
- 1 cup sugar
  Pinch of fine sea salt
- One 4-inch piece vanilla bean
- 1 tablespoon whole black peppercorns
- 4 ripe Anjou or Bartlett pears

❖ CHEF'S SECRET: Poaching means that a liquid is simmering; look for tiny bubbles visible in the pan. Large bubbles are an indication that the heat is too high.

Big Five

SEASONAL FIVE-COURSE MENUS

❖ SUMMER

*Linguine con La Salsa
di Noci*

LINGUINI WITH WALNUT SAUCE

Pollo al Limone ed Erbe

ROAST CHICKEN WITH LEMON
AND HERBS

Zucchine all'arrabiata

HOT AND SPICY ZUCCHINI COINS

*Insalata di Radicchio
Ricotta Salata e Albicocche*

RADICCIO, RICOTTA SALATA, AND
DRIED APRICOT SALAD

Torta di Gelato

GELATO PIE

❖ FALL

*Crema di Broccolo
e Zucchine*

CREAM OF BROCCOLI AND
ZUCCHINI SOUP

*Cotolette di Maiale
al Pistacchio*

PISTACHIO-DUSTED PORK CHOPS

Patate in Casseruola

POTATO CASSEROLE

Insalata di Sedano e Funghi

CELERY AND MUSHROOM SALAD

Crostata di Marmellata

JAM TART

❖ WINTER

Fonduta

ITALIAN CHEESE FONDUE

Minestra di Spinaci

SPINACH SOUP

*Bistecca con Salsa di
Capperi*

STEAK WITH CAPER SAUCE

*Insalata di Barbabietola ed
Arance*

BEET AND ORANGE SALAD

*Mele Infornate con le Noci
e Marmellata*

BAKED APPLES WITH NUTS AND
MARMALADE

❖ SPRING

Gnocchetti al Prezzemolo

LITTLE PARSELY GNOCCHI

*Abbacchio al Forno alla
Romana*

ROAST LAMB, ROMAN STYLE

Insalata di Cavolfiore

CAULIFLOWER SALAD

Insalata Scarola

ESCAROLE SALAD WITH MUSTARD
DRESSING

Panna Cotta con Vaniglia

BUTTERMILK PANNA COTTA
WITH VANILLA

Index